Sweeney Todd

The Demon Barber OF FLEET STREET

Sweeney Todd
The Demon Barber of Fleet Street

A MUSICAL THRILLER

MUSIC AND LYRICS BY

STEPHEN SONDHEIM

BOOK BY

HUGH WHEELER

BASED ON A VERSION OF "SWEENEY TODD" BY

CHRISTOPHER BOND

PRODUCTION DIRECTED BY

HAROLD PRINCE

DODD, MEAD & COMPANY · NEW YORK

To Flora and Janet Roberts

No part of this book may be reproduced in any form
without permission in writing from the publisher.
Published by Dodd, Mead & Company, Inc.
79 Madison Avenue, New York, N.Y. 10016
Distributed in Canada by
McClelland and Stewart Limited, Toronto
Manufactured in the United States of America
Third Printing

Library of Congress Cataloging in Publication Data

Sondheim, Stephen
Sweeney Todd. Libretto. English.
  Sweeney Todd
  1. Musical revues, comedies, etc.—Librettos.
  I. Wheeler, Hugh Callingham— Sweeney Todd
  II. Title
ML50.S705S9   1979   782.8'1'2   79-18468
ISBN 0-396-07776-5
ISBN 0-396-08598-9 (pbk.)

SWEENEY TODD, THE DEMON BARBER OF FLEET STREET *was first presented on March 1, 1979, by Richard Barr, Charles Woodward, Robert Fryer, Mary Lea Johnson, Martin Richards, in association with Dean and Judy Manos, at the Uris Theatre, New York City, with the following cast:*

ANTHONY HOPE	*Victor Garber*
SWEENEY TODD	*Len Cariou*
BEGGAR WOMAN	*Merle Louise*
MRS. LOVETT	*Angela Lansbury*
JUDGE TURPIN	*Edmund Lyndeck*
THE BEADLE	*Jack Eric Williams*
JOHANNA	*Sarah Rice*
TOBIAS RAGG	*Ken Jennings*
PIRELLI	*Joaquin Romaguera*
JONAS FOGG	*Robert Ousley*

The Company

Duane Bodin, Walter Charles, Carole Doscher, Nancy Eaton, Mary-Pat Green, Cris Groenendaal, Skip Harris, Marthe Ihde, Betsy Joslyn, Nancy Killmer, Frank Kopyc, Spain Logue, Craig Lucas, Pamela McLernon, Duane Morris, Robert Ousley, Richard Warren Pugh, Maggie Task (Swings—Heather B. Withers, Robert Hendersen).

Dance and Movement by LARRY FULLER
Production designed by EUGENE LEE
Costumes by FRANNE LEE
Lighting designed by KEN BILLINGTON
Orchestrations by JONATHAN TUNICK
Musical direction by PAUL GEMIGNANI

MUSICAL NUMBERS

ACT ONE

"The Ballad of Sweeney Todd"   *Company*

"No Place Like London"   *Anthony, Todd, Beggar Woman*

"The Barber and His Wife"   *Todd*

"The Worst Pies in London"   *Mrs. Lovett*

"Poor Thing"   *Mrs. Lovett*

"My Friends"   *Todd, Mrs. Lovett*

"Green Finch and Linnet Bird"   *Johanna*

"Ah, Miss"   *Anthony, Beggar Woman*

"Johanna"   *Anthony*

"Pirelli's Miracle Elixir"   *Tobias, Todd, Mrs. Lovett,*
                                                          Company

"The Contest"   *Pirelli*

"Wait"   *Mrs. Lovett*

"Kiss Me"   *Johanna, Anthony*

"Ladies in Their Sensitivities"   *The Beadle*

Quartet   *Johanna, Anthony, The Beadle,*
                                                  Judge Turpin

"Pretty Women"   *Todd, Judge Turpin*

"Epiphany"   *Todd*

"A Little Priest"   *Todd, Mrs. Lovett*

ACT TWO

THE PLACE
London: Fleet Street and environs

THE TIME
The 19th Century

Sweeney Todd

The Demon Barber of Fleet Street

PROLOGUE

As the audience enters, an organist takes his place at a huge eccentric organ to the side of the stage and begins to play funeral music. Before a front drop two gravediggers appear, carrying shovels, and begin to dig a grave downstage center. As they dig they disappear six feet into the earth, leaving piles of dirt on the upstage side.

At curtain time a police warden appears, looks at his watch, hurrying them. Two workmen enter. They pull down the drop. The deafeningly shrill sound of a factory whistle. Blackout.

The lights come up to reveal the company. A man steps forward and sings.

MAN
Attend the tale of Sweeney Todd.
His skin was pale and his eye was odd.
He shaved the faces of gentlemen
Who never thereafter were heard of again.
He trod a path that few have trod,

Did Sweeney Todd,
The Demon Barber of Fleet Street.

ANOTHER MAN
He kept a shop in London town,
Of fancy clients and good renown.
And what if none of their souls were saved?
They went to their maker impeccably shaved
By Sweeney,
By Sweeney Todd,
The Demon Barber of Fleet Street.
> (A *blinding light cuts down the stage as an up-
> stage iron door opens. Two men enter. They
> carry a body in a bag, tied at both ends with rope.
> They are followed by a woman carrying a tin
> canister marked "Flour." They walk to the edge
> of the grave and unceremoniously dump the
> body in it. The woman opens the canister and
> pours black ashes into the hole. This action cov-
> ers the next verse of the song*)

COMPANY
Swing your razor wide, Sweeney!
Hold it to the skies!
Freely flows the blood of those
Who moralize!
> (*Various members of the company step forward
> and sing*)

SOLOISTS
His needs were few, his room was bare:
A lavabo and a fancy chair,
A mug of suds and a leather strop,

An apron, a towel, a pail and a mop.
For neatness he deserves a nod,
Does Sweeney Todd,

COMPANY
The Demon Barber of Fleet Street.

WOMEN
Inconspicuous Sweeney was,
Quick and quiet and clean 'e was.
Back of his smile, under his word,
Sweeney heard music that nobody heard.
Sweeney pondered and Sweeney planned,
Like a perfect machine 'e planned.
Sweeney was smooth, Sweeney was subtle,
Sweeney would blink and rats would scuttle.
   (*The men join in singing, voices overlapping, in
   a gradual crescendo*)
Sweeney was smooth, Sweeney was subtle,
Sweeney would blink and rats would scuttle.
Inconspicuous Sweeney was,
Quick and quiet and clean 'e was,
Like a perfect machine 'e was,
Was Sweeney!
Sweeney!
Sweeney!
Sweeeeeeneeeeeey!
   (TODD *rises out of the grave and sings as the
   company repeats his words*)

TODD *and* COMPANY
Attend the tale of Sweeney Todd.
He served a dark and a vengeful god.

TODD

What happened then—well, that's the play,
And he wouldn't want us to give it away,
Not Sweeney,

TODD *and* COMPANY

Not Sweeney Todd,
The Demon Barber of Fleet Street . . .
   *(The scene blacks out. The bells of a clock tower
   chime. Early morning light comes up)*

ACT I

A street by the London docks. SWEENEY TODD *and* ANTHONY HOPE *enter.* ANTHONY *is a cheerful country-born young ship's first mate with a duffel bag slung over his shoulder.* TODD *is a heavy-set, saturnine man in his forties who might, say, be a blacksmith or a dockhand. There is about him an air of brooding, slightly nerve-chilling self-absorption.*

ANTHONY
(Sings)
I have sailed the world, beheld its wonders
From the Dardanelles
To the mountains of Peru,
But there's no place like London!
I feel home again.

I could hear the city bells
Ring whatever I would do.
No, there's no pl—

TODD
(Sings grimly)
No, there's no place like London.

ANTHONY
(*Speaks, surprised at the interruption*)
Mr. Todd, sir?

TODD
(*Sings*)
You are young.
Life has been kind to you.
You will learn.
(*Speaks, music under*)
It is here we go our several ways. Farewell, Anthony, I will not soon forget the good ship *Bountiful* nor the young man who saved my life.

ANTHONY
There's no cause to thank me for that, sir. It would have been a poor Christian indeed who'd have spotted you pitching and tossing on that raft and not given the alarm.

TODD
There's many a Christian would have done just that and not lost a wink's sleep for it, either.
(*A ragged* BEGGAR WOMAN *suddenly appears*)

BEGGAR WOMAN
(*Approaching, holding out bowl to* ANTHONY, *sings*)
Alms! . . . Alms! . . .
For a miserable woman
On a miserable chilly morning . . .
(ANTHONY *drops a coin in her bowl*)
Thank yer, sir, thank yer.
(*Softly, suddenly leering in a mad way*)
'Ow would you like a little squiff, dear,

A little jig jig,
A little bounce around the bush?
Wouldn't you like to push me crumpet?
It looks to me, dear,
Like you got plenty there to push.
    (As ANTHONY *starts back in embarrassment, she*
    turns instantly and pathetically to TODD, *who*
    tries to keep his back to her)
Alms! . . . Alms! . . .
For a pitiful woman
Wot's got wanderin' wits . . .
Hey, don't I know you, mister?
    (*She peers intently at him*)

TODD

Must you glare at me, woman? Off with you, off, I say!

BEGGAR WOMAN
(*Smiling vacantly*)
Then 'ow would you like to fish me squiff, mister?
We'll go jig jig,
A little—

TODD
(*Making a gesture as if to strike her*)
Off, I said. To the devil with you!
    (*She scuttles away, turns to give him a piercing*
    look, then wanders off)

BEGGAR WOMAN
(*Singing as she goes*)
Alms! . . . Alms! . . .
For a desperate woman . . .
    (*Music continues under*)

ANTHONY
(A *little bewildered*)
Pardon me, sir, but there's no need to fear the likes of
her. She was only a half-crazed beggar woman. London's
full of them.

TODD
(*Half to himself, half to* ANTHONY)
I beg your indulgence, boy. My mind is far from easy, for
in these once-familiar streets I feel the chill of ghostly
shadows everywhere. Forgive me.

ANTHONY
There's nothing to forgive.

TODD
Farewell, Anthony.

ANTHONY
Mr. Todd, before we part—

TODD
(*Suddenly fierce*)
What is it?

ANTHONY
I have honored my promise never to question you.
Whatever brought you to that sorry shipwreck is your
affair. And yet, during those many weeks of the voyage
home, I have come to think of you as friend and, if
trouble lies ahead for you in London . . . if you need
help—or money . . .

TODD
(*Almost shouting*)

No!

(ANTHONY *starts, perplexed;* TODD *makes a placating gesture, sings quietly and intensely*)
There's a hole in the world
Like a great black pit
And the vermin of the world
Inhabit it
And its morals aren't worth
What a pig could spit
And it goes by the name of London.

At the top of the hole
Sit the privileged few,
Making mock of the vermin
In the lower zoo,
Turning beauty into filth and greed.
I too
Have sailed the world and seen its wonders,
For the cruelty of men
Is as wondrous as Peru,
But there's no place like London!
(*Pause, music under, then as if in a trance*)
There was a barber and his wife.
And she was beautiful.
A foolish barber and his wife.
She was his reason and his life,
And she was beautiful.
And she was virtuous.
And he was—
(*Shrugs*)
Naive.

There was another man who saw
That she was beautiful,
A pious vulture of the law
Who with a gesture of his claw
Removed the barber from his plate.
Then there was nothing but to wait
And she would fall,
So soft,
So young,
So lost,
And oh, so beautiful!
                    (*Pauses, music under*)

ANTHONY

And the lady, sir—did she—succumb?

TODD

Oh, that was many years ago . . .
I doubt if anyone would know.
                    (*Speaks, music under*)
Now, leave me, Anthony, I beg of you. There's some-
where I must go, something I must find out. Now. And
alone.

ANTHONY

But surely we will meet again before I'm off to Plymouth!

TODD

If you want, you may well find me. Around Fleet Street,
I wouldn't wonder.

ANTHONY

Well, until then, Mr. Todd.

(ANTHONY *starts off down the street.* TODD *stands a moment alone in thought, then starts down the street in the opposite direction*)

TODD
(*Sings*)
There's a hole in the world
Like a great black pit
And it's filled with people
Who are filled with shit
And the vermin of the world
Inhabit it . . .
(*As* TODD *disappears, we see Mrs. Lovett's Pieshop. Above it is an empty apartment which is reached by an outside staircase.* MRS. LOVETT, *a vigorous, slatternly woman in her forties, is flicking flies off the trays of pies with a dirty rag as she sings or hums.* TODD *appears at the end of the street and moves slowly toward the pieshop, looking around as if remembering. Seeing the pieshop he pauses a moment at some distance, gazing at it and at* MRS. LOVETT, *who has now picked up a wicked-looking knife and starts chopping suet. After a beat,* TODD *moves toward the shop, hesitates and then enters.* MRS. LOVETT *does not notice him until his shadow passes across her. She looks up, knife in air, and screams, freezing him in his tracks*)

MRS. LOVETT
A customer!
(TODD *has started out in alarm.* MRS. LOVETT *sings*)

Wait! What's yer rush? What's yer hurry?
>   (*She sticks the knife into the counter*)
You gave me such a—
>   (*She wipes her hands on her apron*)
Fright. I thought you was a ghost.
Half a minute, can'tcher?
Sit! Sit ye down!
>   (*Forcefully*)
Sit!
All I meant is that I
Haven't seen a customer for weeks.
Did you come here for a pie, sir?
>   (TODD *nods. She flicks a bit of dust off a pie with*
>   *her rag*)
Do forgive me if me head's a little vague—
Ugh!
>   (*She plucks something off a pie, holds it up*)
What is *that*?
But you'd think we had the plague—
>   (*She drops it on the floor and stamps on it*)
From the way that people—
>   (*She flicks something off a pie with her finger*)
Keep avoiding—
>   (*Spotting it moving*)
No you don't!
>   (*She smacks it with her hand*)
Heaven knows I try, sir!
>   (*Lifts her hand, looks at it*)
Ick!
>   (*She wipes it on the edge of the counter*)
But there's no one comes in even to inhale—
Tsk!
>   (*She blows the last dust off the pie as she brings*
>   *it to him*)

Right you are, sir. Would you like a drop of ale?

        (TODD *nods*)

Mind you, I can't hardly blame them—

        (*Pouring a tankard of ale*)

These are probably the worst pies in London.
I know why nobody cares to take them—
I should know,
I make them.
But good? No,
The worst pies in London—
Even that's polite.
The worst pies in London—
If you doubt it, take a bite.

        (*He does*)

Is that just disgusting?
You have to concede it.
It's nothing but crusting—
Here, drink this, you'll need it—

        (*She puts the ale in front of him*)

The worst pies in London—

   (*During the following, she slams lumps of
   dough on the counter and rolls them out, grunt-
   ing frequently as she goes*)

And no wonder with the price of
Meat what it is

        (*Grunt*)

When you get it.

        (*Grunt*)

Never

        (*Grunt*)

Thought I'd live to see the day men'd think it was a
Treat finding poor

        (*Grunt*)

Animals

(*Grunt*)

Wot are dying in the street.
Mrs. Mooney has a pie shop,
Does a business, but I notice something weird—
Lately all her neighbors' cats have disappeared.
Have to hand it to her—
Wot I calls
Enterprise,
Popping pussies into pies.
Wouldn't do in my shop—
Just the thought of it's enough to make you sick.
And I'm telling you them pussy cats is quick.
No denying times is hard, sir—
Even harder than
The worst pies in London.
Only lard and nothing more—

(As TODD *gamely tries another mouthful*)

Is that just revolting?
All greasy and gritty,
It looks like it's molting,
And tastes like—
Well, pity
A woman alone
With limited wind
And the worst pies in London!

(*Sighs heavily*)

Ah sir,
Times is hard. Times is hard.

(*She finishes one of the crusts with a flourish,*
then notices TODD *having difficulty with his pie*)

Spit it out, dear. Go on. On the floor. There's worse
things than that down there.

(As *he does*)

That's my boy.

TODD

Isn't that a room up there over the shop? If times are so hard, why don't you rent it out? That should bring in something.

MRS. LOVETT

Up there? Oh, no one will go near it. People think it's haunted. You see—years ago, something happened up there. Something not very nice.
(*Sings*)
There was a barber and his wife,
And he was beautiful,
A proper artist with a knife,
But they transported him for life.
(*Sighs*)
And he was beautiful . . .
(*Speaks, music continuing under*)
Barker, his name was—Benjamin Barker.

TODD

Transported? What was his crime?

MRS. LOVETT

Foolishness.
(*Sings*)
He had this wife, you see,
Pretty little thing.
Silly little nit
Had her chance for the moon on a string—
Poor thing. Poor thing.
(*As she sings, her narration is acted out. First we see the pretty young* WIFE *in the empty upstairs room dancing her household chores. During the following the* JUDGE *and his obsequious assistant, the* BEADLE, *approach the house, gazing up*

at the WIFE *lecherously. The* WIFE *remains de-
mure, sewing)*
There were these two, you see,
Wanted her like mad,
One of 'em a judge,
T'other one his beadle.
Every day they'd nudge
And they'd wheedle.
But she wouldn't budge
From her needle.
Too bad. Pure thing.
*(Far upstage, in very dim light, shapes appear. A
swirl of cloth, glints of jewels, the faces of people
masked as animals and demons. During the fol-
lowing lyric, the* WIFE *takes an imaginary baby
from an imaginary cot and sits on the floor,
cradling it in her arms as she sobs)*
So they merely shipped the poor bugger off south,
they did,
Leaving her with nothing but grief and a year-old kid.
Did she use her head even then? Oh no, God forbid!
Poor fool.
Ah, but there was worse yet to come—
(Intake of breath)
Poor thing.
*(Again the shapes appear, this time a bit more
distinctly.* MRS. LOVETT *speaks, musingly)*
Johanna, that was the baby's name. . . Pretty little
Johanna. . .
(Drifts off in reminiscence)

TODD
(Tensely)

Go on.

MRS. LOVETT

(*Eyeing* TODD *sharply*)

My, you do like a good story, don't you?

(*The* BEADLE *reappears, gazing up at the* WIFE, *miming in a solicitous manner for her to come down.* MRS. LOVETT, *warming to the tale, sings*)

Well, Beadle calls on her, all polite,
Poor thing, poor thing.
The Judge, he tells her, is all contrite,
He blames himself for her dreadful plight,
She must come straight to his house tonight!
Poor thing, poor thing.

(*Excited, almost gleeful*)

Of course, when she goes there,
Poor thing, poor thing.
They're havin' this ball all in masks.

(*The shapes are now clear. A ball is in progress at the* JUDGE'S *house: the company, wearing grotesque masks, is dancing a slow minuet. The* BEADLE, *leading the* WIFE, *appears, moving with her through the dancers. He gives her champagne. She looks dazedly around, terrified*)

There's no one she knows there,
Poor dear, poor thing.
She wanders tormented, and drinks,
Poor thing.
The Judge has repented, she thinks,
Poor thing.
"Oh, where is Judge Turpin?" she asks.

(*During the following, the* JUDGE *appears, tears off his mask, then his cloak, revealing himself naked. She screams as he reaches for her, struggling wildly as the* BEADLE *hurls her to the floor. He holds her there as the* JUDGE *mounts her and*

*the masked dancers pirouette around the
ravishment, giggling*)
He was there, all right—
Only not so contrite!
She wasn't no match for such craft, you see,
And everyone thought it so droll.
They figured she had to be daft, you see,
So all of 'em stood there and laughed, you see.
Poor soul!
Poor thing!

TODD
(A *wild shout*)
Would no one have mercy on her?
(*The dumb show vanishes.* TODD *and* MRS.
LOVETT *gaze at each other*)

MRS. LOVETT
(*Coolly*)
So it is you—Benjamin Barker.

TODD
(*Frighteningly vehement*)
Not Barker! Not Barker! Todd now! Sweeney Todd!
Where is she?

MRS. LOVETT
So changed! Good God, what did they do to you down
there in bloody Australia or wherever?

TODD
Where is my wife? Where's Lucy?

MRS. LOVETT

She poisoned herself. Arsenic from the apothecary on the corner. I tried to stop her but she wouldn't listen to me.

TODD

And my daughter?

MRS. LOVETT

Johanna? He's got her.

TODD

He? Judge Turpin?

MRS. LOVETT

Even he had a conscience tucked away, I suppose. Adopted her like his own. You could say it was good luck for her . . . almost.

TODD

Fifteen years sweating in a living hell on a trumped up charge. Fifteen years dreaming that, perhaps, I might come home to a loving wife and child.
(TODD *strikes ferociously on the pie counter with his fists*)
Let them quake in their boots—Judge Turpin and the Beadle—for their hour has come.

MRS. LOVETT
(Awed)

You're going to—get 'em? You? A bleeding little nobody of a runaway convict? Don't make me laugh. You'll

never get His 'igh and Mightiness! Nor the Beadle
neither. Not in a million years.
>   (*No reaction from* TODD)
You got any money?
>   (*Still no reaction*)
Listen to me! You got any money?

TODD

No money.

MRS. LOVETT

Then how you going to live even?

TODD

I'll live. If I have to sweat in the sewers or in the plague
hospital, I'll live—and I'll have them.

MRS. LOVETT

Oh, you poor thing! You poor thing!
>   (*A sudden thought*)
Wait!
> (*She disappears behind a curtained entrance
> leading to her parlor. For a beat* TODD *stands
> alone, almost exalted.* MRS. LOVETT *returns with
> a razor case. She holds it out to him*)

See! It don't have to be the sewers or the plague hospital.
When they come for the little girl, I hid 'em. I thought,
who knows? Maybe the poor silly blighter'll be back again
someday and need 'em. Cracked in the head, wasn't I?
Times as bad as they are, I could have got five, maybe
ten quid for 'em, any day. See? You can be a barber
again.
> (*Music begins. She opens the case for him to look*

inside. TODD *stands a long moment gazing down at the case)*
My, them handles is chased silver, ain't they?

TODD

Silver, yes.
      (Quietly, looking into the box, sings)
These are my friends.
See how they glisten.
        (Picks up a small razor)
See this one shine,
How he smiles in the light.
My friend, my faithful friend.
    (Holding it to his ear, feeling the edge with his thumb)
Speak to me, friend.
Whisper, I'll listen.
        (Listening)
I know, I know—
You've been locked out of sight
All these years—
Like me, my friend.

Well, I've come home
To find you waiting.
Home,
And we're together,
And we'll do wonders,
Won't we?
    (MRS. LOVETT, who has been looking over his shoulder, starts to feel his other ear lightly, absently, in her own trance. TODD lays the razor back in the box and picks out a larger one. They sing simultaneously)

TODD

You there, my friend.
Come, let me hold you.

Now, with a sigh
You grow warm
In my hand,
My friend,
My clever friend.
    (*Putting it back*)
Rest now, my friends.
Soon I'll unfold you.
Soon you'll know splendors
You never have dreamed
All your days,
My lucky friends.
Till now your shine
Was merely silver.
Friends,
You shall drip rubies,
You'll soon drip precious
Rubies . . .

MRS. LOVETT

I'm your friend too, Mr. Todd.
If you only knew, Mr. Todd—
Ooh, Mr. Todd,
You're warm
In my hand.
You've come home.
Always had a fondness for you,
I did.

Never you fear, Mr. Todd,
You can move in here, Mr. Todd.
Splendors you never have dreamed
All your days
Will be yours.
I'm your friend.
Don't they shine beautiful?
Silver's good enough for me,
Mr. T. . . .

(TODD *holds up the biggest razor to the light as the music soars sweetly, then stops. He speaks into the silence*)

TODD

My right arm is complete again!
(*Lights dim except for a scalding spot on the razor as music blares forth from both the organ and the orchestra. The* COMPANY, *including the* JUDGE *and the* BEADLE, *appears and sings*)

COMPANY
Lift your razor high, Sweeney!
Hear it singing, "Yes!"
Sink it in the rosy skin
Of righteousness!
(*Variously*)
His voice was soft, his manner mild.
He seldom laughed but he often smiled.
He'd seen how civilized men behave.
He never forgot and he never forgave,
Not Sweeney,
Not Sweeney Todd,
The Demon Barber of Fleet Street . . .

(*They disappear. There is a moment of darkness
in which we hear the trilling and twittering of
songbirds. Light comes up on the facade of
JUDGE TURPIN's mansion. A BIRD SELLER enters
carrying a bizarre construction of little wicker
birdcages tied together. It is in these that the
birds are singing. At an upper level of the
JUDGE's mansion appears a very young, exqui-
sitely beautiful girl with a long mane of shining
blonde hair. This is JOHANNA. For a moment she
stands disconsolate, then her eyes fall on the
birds*)

JOHANNA
And how are they today?

BIRD SELLER
Hungry as always, Miss Johanna.
(*He lifts the cages up to her*)

JOHANNA
(*Sings*)

Green finch and linnet bird,
Nightingale, blackbird,
How is it you sing?
How can you jubilate,
Sitting in cages,
Never taking wing?
Outside the sky waits,
Beckoning, beckoning,
Just beyond the bars.
How can you remain,
Staring at the rain,
Maddened by the stars?
How is it you sing anything?
How is it you sing?

Green finch and linnet bird,
Nightingale, blackbird,
How is it you sing?
Whence comes this melody constantly flowing?
Is it rejoicing or merely halloing?
Are you discussing or fussing
Or simply dreaming?
Are you crowing?
Are you screaming?

Ringdove and robinet,
Is it for wages,
Singing to be sold?
Have you decided it's
Safer in cages,
Singing when you're told?

(ANTHONY *enters. Instantly he sees her and
stands transfixed by her beauty*)
My cage has many rooms,
Damask and dark.
Nothing there sings,
Not even my lark.
Larks never will, you know,
When they're captive.
Teach me to be more adaptive.

Green finch and linnet bird,
Nightingale, blackbird,
Teach me how to sing.
If I cannot fly,
Let me sing.
(*She gazes into the middle distance disconso-
lately*)

ANTHONY
(*Gazing at her, sings softly*)
I have sailed the world,
Beheld its wonders,
From the pearls of Spain
To the rubies of Tibet,
But not even in London
Have I seen such a wonder . . .
(*Breathlessly*)
Lady look at me look at me miss oh
Look at me please oh
Favor me favor me with your glance.
Ah, miss,
What do you what do you see off

There in those trees oh
Won't you give won't you give me a chance?

Who would sail to Spain
For all its wonders,
When in Kearney's Lane
Lies the greatest wonder yet?

Ah, miss,
Look at you look at you pale and
Ivory-skinned oh
Look at you looking so sad so queer.
Promise
Not to retreat to the darkness
Back of your window
Not till you not till you look down here.
Look at

ANTHONY	JOHANNA
Me!	Green finch and linnet bird,
Look at	Nightingale, blackbird,
Me!	Teach me how to sing.
	If I cannot fly,
Look at me . . .	Let me sing . . .

(As JOHANNA *turns back to go inside, their eyes
meet and the song dies on their lips. A hushed
moment. Then suddenly a clawlike hand darts
out from a pile of trash.* ANTHONY *jumps and
looks down to see the* BEGGAR WOMAN, *who has
been sleeping in the garbage under a discarded
shawl, thrusting her bowl at him.* JOHANNA,
frightened, slips back out of sight)

BEGGAR WOMAN
(*Sings*)
Alms! . . . Alms! . . .
For a miserable woman . . .
    (ANTHONY *hurriedly digs out a coin and drops it
    in her bowl; she peers at him*)
Beg your pardon, it's you, sir . . .
Thank yer . . . Thank yer kindly . . .
    (ANTHONY *turns back to discover* JOHANNA *gone
    and the window shut. The* BEGGAR WOMAN *starts
    off*)

ANTHONY
One moment, mother.
    (*She turns*)
Perhaps you know whose house this is?

BEGGAR WOMAN
That! That's the great Judge Turpin's house, that is.

ANTHONY
And the young lady who resides there?

BEGGAR WOMAN
Ah, her! That's Johanna, his pretty little ward.
    (*Slyly confidential*)
But don't you go trespassing there, young man. Not if
you value your hide.
    (*She nods her head*)
Tamper there and it's a good whipping for you—or any
other youth with mischief on his mind.
    (*Leers at him, sings*)
Hey! Hoy! Sailor boy!

Want it snugly harbored?
Open me gate, but dock it straight,
I see it lists to starboard.
> (*She grabs at his crotch and starts to dance around him grotesquely, lifting her skirts.* AN-THONY *is appalled. He pulls coins out of his pocket and tosses them to her*)

ANTHONY

Here and here and here. Take it and off with you. Off!
> (*The* BEGGAR WOMAN, *cackling, collects the coins and scampers off.* ANTHONY *turns back to the house, gazes up at the window. The noise has frightened the birds, who start screeching.* AN-THONY *becomes aware of them and moves over to the now sleeping* BIRD SELLER, *shakes him awake, and inspects the cages*)

Which one sings the sweetest?

BIRD SELLER

All's the same, sir. Six pence and cheap at the price.
> (ANTHONY *selects one, gives the man a coin, holds up the cage*)

ANTHONY

He sings bravely.
> (*Watches the cage*)

But why does he batter his wings so wildly against the bars?

BIRD SELLER

We blind 'em, sir. That's what we always does. Blind 'em and, not knowing night from day, they sing and sing without stopping, pretty creatures.

(He gets up, slinging the cages on his back, and starts off)

Have pleasure of the bird, sir.

(He exits. JOHANNA *reappears at the window.* AN-THONY *holds up the cage, indicating it is a present and she should come down to get it. She hesitates, smiles, nods, disappears from the window. He waits. Shyly, almost furtively,* JOHANNA *slips out of the door and stands there. He moves toward her, holding out the cage. Slowly her hand goes out toward him. Their fingers touch)*

ANTHONY
(Sings softly)

I feel you,
Johanna,
I feel you.
I was half convinced I'd waken,
Satisfied enough to dream you.
Happily I was mistaken,
Johanna!
I'll steal you,
Johanna,
I'll steal you . . .

(They stand so absorbed with each other that they do not notice the approach of JUDGE TUR-PIN, *followed by the* BEADLE)

JUDGE
(Shouting)

Johanna! Johanna!

30

JOHANNA

Oh dear!
> (*Forgetting the bird cage,* JOHANNA *scurries toward the house.* ANTHONY *turns to find the* JUDGE *glaring at him*)

JUDGE

If I see your face again on this or any other neighbor street, you'll rue the day you were born. Is that plain enough speaking for you?

ANTHONY

But, sir, I swear to you there was nothing in my heart but the most respectful sentiments of—

JUDGE
> (*To* BEADLE)

Dispose of him!
> (*He strides toward the house*)

JOHANNA

Oh dear! I knew!

BEADLE
> (*Fondling the truncheon, to* ANTHONY)

You heard His Worship.

ANTHONY

But, friend, I have no fight with you.
> (*The* BEADLE *takes the cage from him, opens its door, takes out the bird, wrings its neck and then tosses it away*)

BEADLE

Get the gist of it, friend? Next time it'll be *your* neck!
(*He starts after the* JUDGE *and* JOHANNA)

JUDGE

Johanna, if I were to think you encouraged that young
rogue . . .

JOHANNA

Oh father, I hope always to be obedient to your com-
mands.

JUDGE
(*Relenting, patting her cheek*)
Dear child.
(*Gazing at her lustfully*)
How sweet you look in that light muslin gown.
(*She runs into the house, the* JUDGE *after her.
The* BEADLE *follows.* ANTHONY *is left alone, the
empty cage in his hand*)

ANTHONY

I'll steal you,
Johanna,
I'll steal you!
Do they think that walls can hide you?
Even now I'm at your window.
I am in the dark beside you,
Buried sweetly in your yellow hair.
I feel you,
Johanna,
And one day
I'll steal you.

Till I'm with you then,
I'm with you there,
Sweetly buried in your yellow hair . . .
(*He smashes the cage, throws it away and exits.
Light fades on him and comes up to reveal St.
Dunstan's Marketplace. A hand-drawn caravan,
painted like a Sicilian donkey cart, stands on
the street. On its side is written in ornate script:*
SIGNOR ADOLFO PIRELLI HAIRCUTTER-BARBER-
TOOTHPULLER TO HIS ROYAL MAJESTY
THE KING OF NAPLES
and under this:
BANISH BALDNESS WITH PIRELLI'S
MIRACLE ELIXIR
(*The* BEADLE *is strolling around, pompously pa-
trolling his district.* TODD *and* MRS. LOVETT
enter. TODD *is carrying his razor case.* MRS.
LOVETT *has a shopping basket*)

TODD
(*Pointing at the caravan*)
That's him? Over there?

MRS. LOVETT
Yes, dear. He's always here Thursdays.

TODD
(*Reading the sign*)
Haircutter, barber, toothpuller to His Royal Majesty the
King of Naples.

MRS. LOVETT
Eyetalian. All the rage, he is.

TODD

Not for long.

MRS. LOVETT

Oh Mr. T., you really think you can do it?

TODD

By tomorrow they'll all be flocking after me like sheep to be shorn.

MRS. LOVETT
(Sees BEADLE)

Oh no! Look. The Beadle—Beadle Bamford.

TODD

So much the better.

MRS. LOVETT

But what if he recognizes you? Hadn't we better—?

TODD

I will do what I have set out to do, woman.

MRS. LOVETT

Oops. Sorry, dear, I'm sure.
(TOBIAS, PIRELLI's *adolescent, simple-minded assistant, appears through a curtain at the rear of the caravan, beating on a tin drum. A factory whistle blows and a crowd of people comes running on, gathering around him*)

TOBIAS
(Sings)

Ladies and gentlemen!

May I have your attention, perlease?
Do you wake every morning in shame and despair
To discover your pillow is covered with hair
Wot ought not to be there?

Well, ladies and gentlemen,
From now on you can waken at ease.
You need never again have a worry or care,
I will show you a miracle marvelous rare.
Gentlemen, you are about to see something wot rose
     from the dead!
     (A *woman gasps—he smiles and wiggles his*
     finger "no")
On the top of my head.

Scarcely a month ago, gentlemen,
I was struck with a 'orrible
Dermatologic disease.
Though the finest physicians in London were called,
I awakened one morning amazed and appalled
To discover with dread that my head was as bald
As a novice's knees.
I was dying of shame
Till a gentleman came,
An illustrious barber, Pirelli by name.
He give me a liquid as precious as gold,
I rubbed it in daily like wot I was told,
And behold!
     (*Doffs his cap dramatically, revealing moun-*
     tains of hair which cascade to his shoulders)
Only thirty days old!

'Twas Pirelli's
Miracle Elixir,

That's wot did the trick, sir,
True, sir, true.
Was it quick, sir?
Did it in a tick, sir,
Just like an elixir
Ought to do!
   (*To* 1ST MAN)
How about a bottle, mister?
Only costs a penny, guaranteed.

CROWD
(*Simultaneously*)

1ST MAN: Penny buys a bottle, I don't know . . .
2ND MAN: You don't need—
1ST MAN: Ah, let's go! (*Starts to leave*)
TOBIAS: (*To* 3RD MAN) Go ahead and tug, sir.
3RD MAN: Penny for a bottle, is it?
TOBIAS: Go ahead, sir, harder . . .

TOBIAS
(*Stopping the* 1ST MAN, *who's quite bald, by pouring a drop on his head*)
Does Pirelli's
Stimulate the growth, sir?
You can have my oath, sir,
'Tis unique.
   (*Takes the man's hand and gently applies it to the wet spot*)
Rub a minute.
Stimulatin', i'n' it?
Soon you'll have to thin it
Once a week!
Penny buys a bottle, guaranteed!

CROWD
(*Simultaneously*)

1ST MAN: (*To* 2ND MAN) Penny buys a bottle, might as well . . . (*Looks hesitantly to* 2ND MAN)

3RD MAN: Wotcher think?

2ND WOMAN: Go ahead and try it, wot the hell . . .

TOBIAS: (*To others*) How about a sample? Have you ever smelled a cleaner smell?

1ST WOMAN: (*To* 3RD MAN) Isn't it a crime they let these urchins clog the pavement?

4TH MAN: Penny buys a bottle, does it?

TOBIAS: (*To* 2ND MAN) That's enough, sir, ample.

TOBIAS

Gently dab it.
Gets to be a habit.
Soon there'll be enough, sir,
Somebody can grab it.
          (*Points to a man standing nearby*)
See that chap with
Hair like Shelley's?
You can tell 'e's
Used Pirelli's!

CROWD
(*Simultaneously*)

1ST MAN: Let me have a bottle.

2ND MAN: Make that two.
     (1ST MAN *buys bottles for both, gets change*)

3RD WOMAN: Come to think of it, I could get some for Harry . . .

4TH WOMAN:	Nothing works on Harry, dear. Bye bye.
TOBIAS:	Go ahead and feel, mum. Absolutely real, mum . . .
2ND MAN:	(*To* 1ST MAN) How about a beer?
1ST MAN:	You know a pub?
2ND MAN:	There's one close by.
1ST WOMAN:	(*To* 2ND WOMAN) You got all the hair you need now.
3RD MAN:	That's no lie.
4TH MAN:	Pass it by.
2ND WOMAN:	I'm just passing by.

TODD

(*Loudly to* MRS. LOVETT)

Pardon me, ma'am, what's that awful stench?

MRS. LOVETT

Are we standing near an open trench?

TODD

Must be standing near an open trench.

TOBIAS

Buy Pirelli's Miracle Elixir:
Anything wot's slick, sir,
Soon sprouts curls.
Try Pirelli's!
When they see how thick, sir,
You can have your pick, sir,
Of the girls!
        (*To* 4TH WOMAN)
Want to buy a bottle, missus?

CROWD
(*Simultaneously*)

TODD: (*Sniffing* 1ST MAN's *bottle*)
What is this?

MRS. LOVETT: (*Examining* 3RD MAN's *bottle*)
What is this?

1ST MAN: Propagates the hair, sir.

4TH MAN: I'll take one!

TODD: (*Hands bottle back distastefully*)
Smells like piss.

MRS. LOVETT: Smells like—phew!

2ND MAN: He says it smells like piss.

TODD: Looks like piss.

MRS. LOVETT: Wouldn't touch it if I was you, dear!

2ND MAN: (*To* 3RD MAN) Wotcher think?

TODD: (*Nods*) This is piss. Piss with ink.

5TH MAN *and*
WOMEN: Says it smells like piss or something.

TOBIAS: Penny for a bottle . . .
Have you ever smelled a cleaner
smell?
How about a sample? . . .
How about a sample, mister? . . .

1ST WOMAN: Give us back our money!

2ND WOMAN: Give us back our money!

1ST WOMAN: Did you ever—?
Give us back our money!

3RD WOMAN: Glad I didn't buy one, I can tell you!

4TH WOMAN: (*To* TOBIAS) If you think that piss can
fool a lady, you're mistaken!

MRS. LOVETT: Give 'em back their money!
Did you ever—?
Give 'em back their money!

3RD WOMAN: Give 'em back their money, I say!
               Give 'em back their money!

TOBIAS: (*Trying to calm them, gesturing to*
                   TODD)
               Never mind that madman, mis-
               ter . . .
               Never mind the madman . . .

TODD *and* MRS. LOVETT

Where is this Pirelli?

CROWD

Where is this Pirelli?
          (*Variously, simultaneously*)
What about my money, laddie?
Yes, what about the money?
Hand it back!
We don't want no piss, boy!
Give it here . . .

TOBIAS

(*Desperately, beating the drum out of rhythm*)
Let Pirelli's
Activate your roots, sir—

TODD

Keep it off your boots, sir—
Eats right through.

CROWD

Go and get Pirelli!

TOBIAS

Yes, get Pirelli's!
Use a bottle of it!
Ladies seem to love it—

MRS. LOVETT

Flies do, too!
     (*Crowd laughs uproariously*)

CROWD

Hand the bloody money over!
Hand the bloody money over!

TOBIAS

    (*Frenetically fast, looking desperately toward the curtain*)
See Pirelli's
Miracle Elixir
Grow a little wick, sir,
Then some fuzz.
The Pirelli's
Soon'll make it thick, sir,
Like a good elixir
Always does!

Trust Pirelli's!
If your hair is sick, sir,
Fix it in the nick, sir,
Don't look grim.
Just Pirelli's
Miracle Elixir,
That'll do the trick, sir—

1ST MAN
What about the money?

TOBIAS
If you've got a kick, sir—

CROWD
(*Individuals, building to a shout*)
What about the money?
Where is this Pirelli?
Go and get Pirelli!
What about our money?

TOBIAS
Tell it to the mixer
Of the Miracle Elixir—
If you've got a kick, sir—!
  (*Desperately yanks the curtain aside, revealing*
  PIRELLI, *an excessively flamboyant Italian with
  a glittering suit, thick wavy hair and a dazzling
  smile—the crowd falls silent, stunned.* TOBIAS
  collapses, exhausted)
Talk to him!

PIRELLI
(*Bows and poses splendidly for a moment, in
one hand an ornate razor, in the other a sinister-
looking tooth-extractor; sings*)
I am Adolfo Pirelli,
Da king of da barbers, da barber of kings,
E buon giorno, good day,
I blow you a kiss!
  (*He does*)

And I, da so-famous Pirelli,
I wish-a to know-a
Who has-a da nerve-a to say
My elixir is piss!
Who says this?

TODD

I do.
                    (*He holds up the bottle of elixir*)
I am Mr. Sweeney Todd and I have opened a bottle of
Pirelli's Elixir, and I say to you it is nothing but an arrant
fraud, concocted from piss and ink.
        (MRS. LOVETT *takes the bottle from* TODD, *sniffs
        it*)

MRS. LOVETT

He's right. Phew! Better to throw your money down the
sewer.
        (*She tosses the bottle to the ground. The onlook-
        ers "ooh and aah" with shocked excitement*)

TOBIAS
        (*Beating agitatedly on the drum, shouting*)
Ladies and gentlemen, pay no attention to that madman.
Who's to be the first for a magnificent shave?

TODD
        (*Breaking in*)
And furthermore . . .
        (*Glaring at* PIRELLI)
I have serviced no kings, yet I wager that I can shave a
cheek and pull a tooth with ten times more dexterity
than any street mountebank!

(He holds up his razor case for the crowd to see)
You see these razors?

MRS. LOVETT
The finest in England.

TODD
(To PIRELLI*)*
I lay them against five pounds you are no match for me.
You hear me, sir? Either accept my challenge or reveal
yourself as a sham.

MRS. LOVETT
Bravo, bravo.
(The crowd laughs and cheers, obviously on
TODD's *side.* PIRELLI, *as imposing as ever, holds
up a hand for silence. Slowly he swaggers toward*
TODD, *takes the razor case, opens it and
examines the razors carefully)*

PIRELLI
*(He speaks with a fairly obvious put-on foreign
accent, barely concealing an Irish underlay)*
Zees are indeed fine razors. Instruments like zees once
seen cannot be soon forgotten.
(Takes out a tooth-extractor)
And a fine extractor, too! You wager zees against five
pounds, sir?

TODD
I do.

PIRELLI
(*Addressing the crowd*)
You hear zis foolish man? Watch and see how he will
regret his folly. Five pounds it is!
(*Music starts*)

TODD
(*Surveying the crowd*)
Friends, neighbors, who's for a free shave?

FIRST MAN
(*Stepping forward eagerly*)
Me, Mr. Todd, sir.

SECOND MAN
(*Stepping forward eagerly, too*)
And me, Mr. Todd, sir.

TODD
Over here. Bring me a chair.

PIRELLI
(*To* TOBIAS)
Boy, bring ze basins, bring ze towels!

TOBIAS
Yes, sir . . .

PIRELLI
Quick!
(*He kicks* TOBIAS. *The boy hurries off into the
caravan*)

TODD

Will Beadle Bamford be the judge?

BEADLE

Glad, as always, to oblige my friends and neighbors.
  (*As another man comes on with a wooden chair
  and* TOBIAS *emerges from the caravan with basins, towels, etc., the* BEADLE *instantly takes
  over. To man, indicating where to set the chair*)
Put it there.
  (1ST MAN *sits on* TODD's *chair. The* 2ND MAN *is
  ensconced on* PIRELLI's *chair.* PIRELLI *shakes out
  a fancy bib with a flourish and covers his man.*
  TODD *takes a towel and tucks it around his
  man's neck*)
Ready?

PIRELLI

Ready!

TODD

Ready!

BEADLE

The fastest, smoothest shave is the winner.
  (*He blows his whistle. The music becomes agitated. The contest begins.* PIRELLI *strops his
  razor quickly,* TODD *in a leisurely manner.*
  PIRELLI *keeps glancing at* TODD *in various
  paranoid ways throughout, frightened of* TODD's
  progress. He starts whipping up lather rapidly)

PIRELLI
(*Sings to crowd while mixing, furiously*)
[Now, signorini, signori,
We mix-a da lather
But first-a you gather
Around, signor-
Ini, signori,
You looking a man
Who have had-a da glory
To shave-a da Pope!
Mr. Sweeney-so-smart—
  (*Sarcastic bow to* TODD)
Oh, I beg-a you pardon—'ll
Call me a lie, was-a only a cardinal—
Nope!
It was-a da Pope!
  (*Looks over shoulder, sees* TODD *still stropping,*
  gains confidence, starts to lather his man's face)
Perhaps, signorini, signori,
You like-a I tell-a
Da famous-a story
Of Queen Isabella,
Da Queen of-a Polan'
Whose toot' was-a swollen,
I pull it so nice from her mout'
That-a though to begin
She's-a screaming-a murder,
She's later-a swoon-a wid
Bliss an' was heard-a
To shout:
"Pull all of 'em out!"]*

* This section was deleted from the New York production.

(*Unexpectedly,* TODD *still shows no sign of starting to shave his man. He merely watches* PIRELLI's *performance.* PIRELLI, *now feeling that he can take the time, sings lyrically as he shaves with rhythmic scrapes and elaborate gestures of wiping the razor*)

To shave-a da face,
To pull-a da toot',
Require da grace
And not-a da brute,
For if-a you slip,
You nick da skin,
You clip-a da chin,
You rip-a da lip a bit
And dat's-a da trut'!

To shave-a da face
Or even a part
Widout it-a smart
Require da heart.
It take-a da art—
I show you a chart—
    (*Pulls down an elaborate chart with many anatomical views of the face and closeups of follicles, etc.*)
I study-a starting in my yout'!
        (TODD *starts slowly mixing his lather*)
To cut-a da hair,
To trim-a da beard,
To make-a da bristle
Clean like a whistle,
Dis is from early infancy

Da talent give to me
By God!
It take-a da skill,
It take-a da brains,
It take-a da will
To take-a da pains,
It take-a da pace,
It take-a da grace—
> (*While* PIRELLI *holds this note elaborately,* TODD, *with a few deft strokes, quickly lathers his man's face, shaves him and signals the* BEADLE *to examine the job*)

BEADLE
(*Blowing whistle*)
The winner is Todd.

MRS. LOVETT
(*Feeling the customer's cheek*)
Smooth as a baby's arse!
> (*The crowd "oohs and ahhs"*)

TODD
(*Looks around*)
And now, who's for a tooth pulling—free without charge!

MAN WITH HEAD TIED UP IN RAG
Me, sir. Me, sir.
> (*He runs to the chair vacated by the shaved man*)

TODD
(*Looking around*)
Who else?

(There is silence from the crowd)

No one?

(Turning to the BEADLE)

Then, sir, since there is no means to test the second skill,
I claim the five pounds!

MRS. LOVETT

To which he is entitled!!

(To crowd)

Right?

(The crowd applauds)

PIRELLI

Wait! One moment. Wait!

(He turns to TOBIAS)

You, boy. Get on that chair.

TOBIAS

(In terror)

Me, Signor? Oh, not a tooth, sir, I beg of you! I ain't got
a twinge—not the tiniest pain. I—

PIRELLI

(Giving him a swinging blow on the cheek)

You do now!

*(Forces him into the chair. Turning to the
crowd)*

We see who is zee victor now. Zis Mister Todd—or the
great Pirelli!

BEADLE

Ready?

PIRELLI

Ready!

TODD

Ready!

> (*The* BEADLE *blows his whistle. While* TODD, *even more nonchalant than before, merely stands by his patient,* PIRELLI *forces open the mouth of* TOBIAS, *brandishing his extractor. He peers in, selects a tooth, thrusts the extractor into the mouth and starts to tug while singing with pretended ease. During the song,* TOBIAS *starts moaning, then screaming—musically*)

PIRELLI
(*Sings*)

To pull-a da toot'
Widout-a da skill
Can damage da root—
> (*As* TOBIAS *squirms*)
Now hold-a da still!
An' if-a you slip
You grip a bit,
You hit da pit of it
Or chip-a da tip
And have-a to fill!

To pull-a da toot'
Widout-a da grace,
You leave-a da space
All over da place.
You try to erase
Widout-a da trace . . .

(*Glaring archly at* TODD)
Sometimes is da case
You even-a kill.
 (TODD *still watches;* PIRELLI *is having trouble,*
 TOBIAS's *wails are becoming louder*)
To hold-a da clamp
Widout-a da cramp,
Wid all dat saliva,
It could-a drive-a
You crazy—!
           (*To* TOBIAS, *who is groaning*)
Don' mutter,
Or back-a you go to da gutter—
           (*To the crowd, forcing a smile*)
My touch is as light as a butter-a
Cup!

I take-a da pains,
I learn-a da art,
I use-a da brains,
I give-a da heart,
I have-a da grace,
I win-a da race—!
 (*While again* PIRELLI *holds the note,* TODD
 *stands watching. Then in one swift move, he
 tugs the rag off his patient's head, neatly opens
 the mouth, looks in, and with a single deft mo-
 tion of the extractor, gives a tiny tug and, turning to the crowd, holds up the extracted tooth.
 The* BEADLE *blows his whistle. The crowd roars
 its approval.* PIRELLI, *cut off again in the middle
 of his high note, sees that* TODD *has extracted his
 customer's tooth, and droops*)
I give-a da up.

MAN
(*Jumping up from chair*)
Not a twinge of pain! Not a twinge!

MRS. LOVETT
The man's a bloody marvel!

BEADLE
(*Beaming at* TODD)
The two-time winner—Mr. Sweeney Todd!
(PIRELLI *leaves the tooth unpulled in* TOBIAS's
mouth and, still retaining his imposing dignity,
moves over to TODD)

PIRELLI
(*With profound bow*)
Sir, I bow to a skill far defter than my own.

TODD
The five pounds.

PIRELLI
(*Produces a rather flamboyant purse, and from it*
takes five pounds)
Here, sir. And may the good Lord smile on you—
(*With a sinister smile*)
—until we meet again. Come, boy.
(*Bows to crowd*)
Signori! Bellissime signorine! Buon giorno! Buon giorno
a tutti!
(*Kicking* TOBIAS *ahead of him, he returns to the*
caravan which TOBIAS, *like a horse, pulls off*)

MRS. LOVETT
(To TODD)
Who'd have thought it, dear! You pulled it off!
(The crowd clusters around TODD)

MAN WITH CAP
Oh, sir, Mr. Todd, sir, do you have an establishment of
your own?

MRS. LOVETT
He certainly does. Sweeney Todd's Tonsorial Parlor—
above my meat pieshop on Fleet Street.
(The BEADLE strolls somewhat menacingly over
to them)

BEADLE
Mr. Todd . . . Strange, sir, but it seems your face is
known to me.

MRS. LOVETT
(Concealing agitation)
Him? That's a laugh—him being my uncle's cousin and
arrived from Birmingham yesterday.

TODD
(Very smooth)
But already, sir, I have heard Beadle Bamford spoken of
with great respect.

BEADLE
(Whatever dim suspicions he may have had al-
layed by the flattery)
Well, sir, I try my best for my neighbors.

(*To* MRS. LOVETT)
Fleet Street? Over your pieshop, ma'am?

MRS. LOVETT
That's it, sir.

BEADLE
Then, Mr. Todd, you will surely see me there before the week is out.

TODD
(*Expressionless*)
You will be welcome, Beadle Bamford, and I guarantee to give you, without a penny's charge, the closest shave you will ever know.
(MRS. LOVETT *takes* TODD's *arm and starts with him offstage as the scene blacks out. In limbo, the* BEGGAR WOMAN *appears with other members of the company. They sing*)

MEMBERS OF THE COMPANY
Sweeney pondered and Sweeney planned.
Like a perfect machine 'e planned,
Barbing the hook, baiting the trap,
Setting it out for the Beadle to snap.

Slyly courted 'im, Sweeney did,
Set a sort of a scene, 'e did.
Laying the trail, showing the traces,
Letting it lead to higher places . . .
Sweeney . . .
(*Light comes up on Mrs. Lovett's Pieshop and the apartment above, which now is sparsely fur-*

nished with a washstand and a long wooden chest. At the foot of the outside staircase is a brand-new barber's pole. Attached to the first banister of the staircase is an iron bell. TODD is pacing in the apartment above. MRS. LOVETT comes hurrying out of the shop, carrying a wooden chair. As she does so, the BEGGAR WOMAN shuffles up to her)

BEGGAR WOMAN
(Sings)
Alms . . . alms . . .

MRS. LOVETT
(Imitating her nastily, singing)
Alms . . . alms . . .
(Music continues)
How many times have I told you? I'll not have trash from the gutter hanging around my establishment!

BEGGAR WOMAN
Not just a penny, dear? Or a pie? One of them pies that give the stomach cramps to half the neighborhood?
(A cackling laugh)
Come on, dear. Have a heart, dear.

MRS. LOVETT
Off. Off with you or you'll get a kick on the rump that'll make your teeth chatter!

BEGGAR WOMAN
Stuck up thing! You and your fancy airs!
(Shuffling off, into the wings)

Alms . . . alms . . .
For a desperate woman . . .
  (*She exits. Music continues.* MRS. LOVETT *rings
  the bell to indicate her approach and starts
  climbing the stairs. At the sound of the bell,
  TODD becomes alert and snatches up a razor. The
  music becomes agitated. As* MRS. LOVETT *appears, he relaxes somewhat.* MRS. LOVETT *is now
  very proprietary towards him*)

                    MRS. LOVETT
It's not much of a chair, but it'll do till you get your fancy
new one. It was me poor Albert's chair, it was. Sat in it all
day long he did, after his leg give out from the dropsy.
        (*Surveying the room, music under*)
Kinda bare, isn't it? I never did like a bare room. Oh,
well, we'll find some nice little knickknacks.

                    TODD
Why doesn't the Beadle come? "Before the week is out,"
that's what he said.

                    MRS. LOVETT
And who says the week's out yet? It's only Tuesday.
        (*As* TODD *paces restlessly, sings*)
  Easy now.
  Hush, love, hush.
  Don't distress yourself,
  What's your rush?
  Keep your thoughts
  Nice and lush.
  Wait.
                (TODD *paces*)

Hush, love, hush.
Think it through.
Once it bubbles,
Then what's to do?
Watch it close.
Let it brew.
Wait.
                    (TODD *grows calmer*)
I've been thinking, flowers—
Maybe daisies—
To brighten up the room.
Don't you think some flowers,
Pretty daisies,
Might relieve the gloom?
                    (As TODD *doesn't respond*)
Ah, wait, love, wait.
                    (*Music continues under*)

                    TODD
                (*Intensely*)
And the Judge? When will I get him?

                MRS. LOVETT
Can't you think of nothing else? Always broodin' away on
yer wrongs what happened heaven knows how many
years ago—
                    (TODD *turns away violently with a hiss*)
Slow, love, slow.
Time's so fast.
Now goes quickly—
See, now it's past!
Soon will come.

Soon will last.
Wait.
(TODD *grows calm again*)
Don't you know,
Silly man,
Half the fun is to
Plan the plan?
All good things come to
Those who can
Wait.
(*Looking around the room*)
Gillyflowers, maybe,
'Stead of daisies . . .
I don't know, though . . .
What do you think?

TODD
(*Docilely*)

Yes.

MRS. LOVETT
(*Gently taking the razor from him*)
Gillyflowers, I'd say. Nothing like a nice bowl of gillies.
(*During this, we have seen* ANTHONY *moving
down the street. He sees the sign and stops. He
goes to the bell and rings it, then starts running
up the stairs. The effect on* TODD *is electric.
Even* MRS. LOVETT, *affected by his tension,
alerts. She hastily gives him back the razor.* AN-
THONY *bursts enthusiastically in*)

TODD

Anthony.

ANTHONY

Mr. Todd. I've paced Fleet Street a dozen times with no
success. But now the sign! In business already.

TODD

Yes.

ANTHONY

I congratulate you.
                    (*Turning to* MRS. LOVETT)
And . . . er . . .

MRS. LOVETT

Mrs. Lovett, sir.

ANTHONY

A pleasure, ma'am. Oh, Mr. Todd, I have so much to tell
you. I have found the fairest and most loving maid that
any man could dream of! And yet there are problems.
She has a guardian so tyrannical that she is kept shut up
from human eye. But now this morning this key fell from
her shuttered window.
                    (*He holds up* JOHANNA's *key*)
The surest sign that Johanna loves me and . . .

MRS. LOVETT

Johanna?

ANTHONY

That's her name, ma'am, and Turpin that of the abom-
inable parent. A judge, it seems. But, as I said, a monstrous tyrant. Oh Mr. Todd, once the Judge has gone to
court, I'll slip into the house and plead with her to fly

with me tonight. Yet when I have her—where can I
bring her till I have hired a coach to speed us home to
Plymouth? Oh Mr. Todd, if I could lodge her here just
for an hour or two!

    (He gazes at the inscrutable TODD)

MRS. LOVETT
(After a beat)

Bring her, dear.

ANTHONY

Oh thank you, thank you, ma'am.
    (To TODD)
I have your consent, Mr. Todd?

TODD
(After a pause)

The girl may come.
    (ANTHONY *grabs his hand and pumps it, then*
    turns to grab MRS. LOVETT*'s)*

ANTHONY

I shall be grateful for this to the grave. Now I must hurry
for surely the Judge is off to the Old Bailey.
    (Turning at the door)
My thanks! A thousand blessings on you both!
    (He hurries out and down the stairs)

MRS. LOVETT

Johanna! Who'd have thought it! It's like Fate, isn't it?
You'll have her back before the day is out.

TODD

For a few hours? Before he carries her off to the other end of England?

MRS. LOVETT

Oh, that sailor! Let him bring her here and then, since you're so hot for a little . . .
(*Makes a throat-cutting gesture*)
. . . that's the throat to slit, dear. Oh Mr. T., we'll make a lovely home for her. You and me. The poor thing! All those years and not a scrap of motherly affection! I'll soon change that, I will, for if ever there was a maternal heart, it's mine.
(*During this speech* PIRELLI, *accompanied by* TOBIAS, *has appeared on the street. They see the sign and start up the stairs without ringing the bell. Now, as* MRS. LOVETT *goes to* TODD *coquettishly,* PIRELLI *and* TOBIAS *suddenly appear at the door.* TODD *pulls violently away from* MRS. LOVETT)

PIRELLI

(*With Italianate bow*)
Good morning, Mr. Todd—and to you, Bellissima Signorina.
(*He kisses* MRS. LOVETT's *hand*)

MRS. LOVETT

Well, 'ow do you do, Signor, I'm sure.

PIRELLI

A little business with Mr. Todd, Signora. Perhaps if you will give the permission?

MRS. LOVETT

Oh yes, indeed, I'll just pop on down to my pies.
(*Surveying* TOBIAS)
Oh lawks, look at it now! Don't look like it's had a kind
word since half past never!
(*Smiling at him*)
What would you say, son, to a nice juicy meat pie, eh?
Your teeth is strong, I hope?

TOBIAS

Oh yes, ma'am.

MRS. LOVETT
(*Taking his hand*)
Then come with me, love.
(*They start down the stairs to the shop*)

PIRELLI

Mr. Todd.

TODD

Signor Pirelli.

PIRELLI
(*Reverting to Irish*)
Ow, call me Danny, Daniel O'Higgins' the name when
it's not perfessional.
(*Looks around the shop*)
Not much, but I imagine you'll pretty it up a bit.
(*Holds out his hand*)
I'd like me five quid back, if'n ya don't mind.

TODD

Why?

(In the shop, MRS. LOVETT pats a stool for TOBIAS
to sit down and hands him a piece of pie. He
starts to eat greedily)

MRS. LOVETT

That's my boy. Tuck in.

PIRELLI

It'll hold me over till your customers start coming. Then
it's half your profits you'll hand over to me every week on
a Friday, share and share alike. All right . . . Mr. Benjamin Barker?

TODD
(Very quiet)

Why do you call me that?

MRS. LOVETT
(Stroking TOBIAS's luxurious locks)

At least you've got a nice full head of hair on you.

TOBIAS

Well, Ma'am, to tell the truth, Ma'am—
(He reaches up and pulls off the "locks" which
are a wig, revealing his own short-cropped hair)
—gets awful 'ot.
(He continues to eat the pie. PIRELLI strolls over
to the washstand, picks up the razor, flicks it
open)

PIRELLI

You don't remember me. Why should you? I was just a
down and out Irish lad you hired for a couple of weeks—
sweeping up hair and such like—

(*Holding up razor*)

but I remember these—and you. Benjamin Barker, later
transported to Botany Bay for life. So, Mr. Todd—is it a
deal or do I run down the street for me pal Beadle Bamford?

(*For a long moment* TODD *stands gazing at him*)

PIRELLI

(*Sings, nastily*)

You t'ink-a you smart,
You foolish-a boy.
Tomorrow you start
In my-a employ!
You unner-a-stan'?
You like-a my plan—?

(*Once again he hits his high note, and once
again he is interrupted—*TODD *knocks the razor
out of his hand and starts, in a protracted strug-
gle, to strangle him*)

TOBIAS

(*Downstairs, unaware of this*)

Oh gawd, he's got an appointment with his tailor. If he's
late and it's my fault—you don't know him!

(*He jumps up and starts out*)

MRS. LOVETT

I wouldn't want to, I'm sure, dear.

(TODD *violently continues with the strangling*)

TOBIAS
(*Calling on the stairs*)
Signor! It's late! The tailor, sir.
(*Remembering*)
Oh, me wig!
(*Runs back for it. Upstairs* TODD *stops dead at the sound of the voice. He looks around wildly, sees the chest, runs to it, opens the lid and then drags* PIRELLI *to it and tumbles him in, slamming the lid shut just as* TOBIAS *enters. It is at this moment that we realize that one of* PIRELLI's *hands is dangling out of the chest*)
Signor, I did like you said. I reminded you . . . the tailor
. . . Ow, he ain't here.

TODD
Signor Pirelli has been called away.

TOBIAS
Where did he go?

TODD
He didn't say. You'd better run after him.

TOBIAS
Oh no, sir. Knowing him, sir, without orders to the contrary, I'd best wait for him *here*.
(*He crosses to the chest and sits down on it, perilously near* PIRELLI's *hand, which he doesn't notice.* TODD *at this moment does, however. Suddenly he is all nervous smiles*)

TODD

So Mrs. Lovett gave you a pie, did she, my lad?

TOBIAS

Oh yes, sir. She's a real kind lady. One whole pie.
(As *he speaks, his hand moves very close to*
PIRELLI's *hand*)

TODD
(*Moving toward him*)
A whole pie, eh? That's a treat. And yet, if I know a
growing boy, there's still room for more, eh?

TOBIAS

I'd say, sir.
(*Patting his stomach*)
An aching void.
(*Once again his hand is on the edge of the chest,
moving toward* PIRELLI's *hand. Slowly now, we
see the fingers of* PIRELLI's *hand stirring, feebly
trying to clutch* TOBIAS's *hand. When it has almost reached him,* TODD *grabs* TOBIAS *up off the
chest*)

TODD

Then why don't you run downstairs and wait for your
master there? There'll be another pie in it for you, I'm
sure.
(*Afterthought*)
And tell Mrs. Lovett to give you a nice big tot of gin.

TOBIAS

Oo, sir! Gin, sir! Thanking you, sir, thanking you kindly.
Gin! You're a Christian indeed, sir!

(*He runs down the stairs to* MRS. LOVETT)
Oh, ma'am, the gentleman says to give me a nice tot of
gin, ma'am.

MRS. LOVETT

Gin, dear? Why not?
(*Upstairs, with great ferocity,* TODD *opens the
chest, grabs* PIRELLI *by the hair, tugs him up
from the chest and slashes his throat as,
downstairs,* MRS. LOVETT *pours a glass of gin
and hands it to* TOBIAS. *He takes it. The tableau
freezes, then fades*)

THREE TENORS
(*Enter and sing*)
His hands were quick, his fingers strong.
It stung a little but not for long.
And those who thought him a simple clod
Were soon reconsidering under the sod,
Consigned there with a friendly prod
From Sweeney Todd,
The Demon Barber of Fleet Street.

See your razor gleam, Sweeney,
Feel how well it fits
As it floats across the throats
Of hypocrites . . .
(*The ballad ends on a crashing chord as the sing-
ers black out and light comes up on* JUDGE TUR-
PIN *in full panoply of wig, robe, etc. He is about
to convict a very young boy*)

JUDGE
This is the fourth time, sir, that you have been brought

before this bench. Though it is my earnest wish ever to temper justice with mercy, your persistent dedication to a life of crime is such an abomination before God and man that I have no alternative but to sentence you to hang by the neck until you are dead.

(*He produces the black cap and puts it on his head. As he does so the condemned prisoner is led away*)

Court adjourned.

(*During the following, the* JUDGE *removes cap, wig, and gown. To the* BEADLE)

It is perhaps remiss of me to close the court so early, but the stench of those miserable wretches at the bar was so offensive to my nostrils I feared my eagerness for fresher air might well impair the soundness of my judgment.

(*Light dims on the court and finds the* JUDGE *and the* BEADLE *now walking down a street together*)

BEADLE

Well, sir, the adjournment is fortunate for me, sir, for it's today we celebrate my sweet little Annie's birthday, and to have her daddy back so soon to hug and kiss her will be her crowning joy on such a happy day.

JUDGE

It is a happy moment for me, too. Walk home with me for I have news for you. In order to shield her from the evils of this world, I have decided to marry Johanna next Monday.

BEADLE

Ah, sir, happy news indeed.

JUDGE

Strange, when I offered myself to her, she showed a certain reluctance. But that's natural enough in a young girl. Now that she has had time for reflection, I'm sure she will greet my proposal in a more sensible frame of mind.

(*Light leaves them and comes up on* JOHANNA *and* ANTHONY *in* JOHANNA's *room. She is pacing in agitation and fear*)

JOHANNA
(*Sings*)

He means to marry me Monday,
What shall I do? I'd rather die.

ANTHONY

I have a plan—

JOHANNA

I'll swallow poison on Sunday,
That's what I'll do, I'll get some lye.

ANTHONY

I have a plan—

JOHANNA
(*Stops pacing suddenly*)

Oh, dear, was that a noise?

ANTHONY

A plan—

JOHANNA

I think I heard a noise.

ANTHONY

A plan!

JOHANNA

It couldn't be,
He's in court,
He's in court today,
Still that was a noise,
Wasn't that a noise?
You must have heard that—

ANTHONY

Kiss me.

JOHANNA
(*Shyly*)

Oh, sir . . .

ANTHONY

Ah, miss . . .

JOHANNA

Oh, sir . . .
(*She turns away, agitatedly*)
If he should marry me Monday,
What shall I do? I'll die of grief.

ANTHONY

We fly tonight—

JOHANNA

'Tis Friday, virtually Sunday,
What can we do with time so brief?

ANTHONY

We fly tonight—

JOHANNA

Behind the curtain—quick!

ANTHONY

Tonight—

JOHANNA

I think I heard a click!

ANTHONY

Tonight!

JOHANNA
It was a gate!
It's the gate!   ANTHONY
We don't have a gate.   It's not a gate.
Still there was a—Wait!   There's no gate,
There's another click!   You don't have a gate.
You must have heard that— If you'd only listen, miss, and—

ANTHONY

Kiss me!

JOHANNA

Tonight?

ANTHONY

Kiss me.

JOHANNA

You mean tonight?

ANTHONY
The plan is made.

JOHANNA
Oh, sir!

ANTHONY
So kiss me.

JOHANNA
I feel a fright.

ANTHONY
Be not afraid.

JOHANNA	ANTHONY
Sir, I did	Tonight I'll
Love you even as I	Steal
Saw you, even as it	You,
Did not matter that I	Johanna,
Did not know your name.	I'll steal you . . .

ANTHONY
It's me you'll marry on Monday,
That's what you'll do!

JOHANNA
And gladly, sir.

ANTHONY
St. Dunstan's, noon.

JOHANNA
I knew I'd be with you one day,
Even not knowing who you were.　　　　ANTHONY
I feared you'd never come,　　　　　　Ah, miss,
That you'd been called away,　　　　　Marry me, marry me, miss,
That you'd been killed,　　　　　　　Oh, marry me Monday!
Had the plague,　　　　　　　　　　Favor me, favor me
Were in debtor's jail,　　　　　　　　With your hand.
Trampled by a horse,　　　　　　　　Promise,
Gone to sea again,　　　　　　　　　Marry me, marry me, please,
Arrested by the—　　　　　　　　　　Oh, marry me Monday—

JOHANNA

Kiss me!

ANTHONY

Of course.

JOHANNA

Quickly!

ANTHONY

You're sure?

JOHANNA

Kiss me!

ANTHONY
(Taking her in his arms)

I shall!

JOHANNA

Kiss me!

Oh, sir . . .
(*Lights dim on them but remain; light rises on the* JUDGE *and the* BEADLE, *still walking together. Music continues under*)

JUDGE
(*Strolling with* BEADLE)
Yes, yes, but surely the respect that she owes me as her guardian should be sufficient to kindle a more tender emotion.

BEADLE
(*Sings*)
Excuse me, my lord.
May I request, my lord,
Permission, my lord, to speak?
Forgive me if I suggest, my lord,
You're looking less than your best, my lord,
There's powder upon your vest, my lord,
And stubble upon your cheek.
And ladies, my lord, are weak.
(*Music continues*)

JUDGE
Perhaps if she greets me cordially upon my return, I should give her a small gift . . .

BEADLE
(*Winces delicately*)
Ladies in their sensitivities, my lord,
Have a fragile sensibility.
When a girl's emergent,
Probably it's urgent
You defer to her gent-

Ility, my lord.
Personal disorder cannot be ignored,
Given their genteel proclivities.
Meaning no offense, it
Happens they resents it,
Ladies in their sensit-
Ivities, my lord.

JUDGE
(Feeling his chin)

Stubble, you say? Perhaps at times I am a little overhasty
with my morning ablutions . . .

BEADLE

Fret not though, my lord,
I know a place, my lord,
A barber, my lord, of skill.
Thus armed with a shaven face, my lord,
Some eau de cologne to brace my lord
And musk to enhance the chase, my lord,
You'll dazzle the girl until
She bows to your every will.

JUDGE

That may well be so.
     (They have reached the JUDGE's *house)*

BEADLE

Well, here we are, Sir. I bid you good day.

JUDGE

Good day.
     (He muses, turns)
And where is this miraculous barber?

BEADLE

In Fleet Street, sir.

JUDGE

Perhaps you may be right. Take me to him.
(*They start off. Light up on* JOHANNA's *room.*
JOHANNA *and* ANTHONY *get up from a couch*)

BEADLE
(*Sings*)

The name is Todd . . .

JUDGE

Todd, eh?

ANTHONY

We'd best not wait until Monday.

JOHANNA
Sir, I concur,   BEADLE
And fully, too.   Sweeney Todd.

ANTHONY

It isn't right.
We'd best be married on Sunday.

JOHANNA

Saturday, sir,
Would also do.

ANTHONY

Or else tonight.
(*The* JUDGE *and the* BEADLE *move past the*
house)

JOHANNA

I think I heard a noise.

ANTHONY

Fear not.

JOHANNA

I mean another noise!

ANTHONY

Like what?

JOHANNA	
Oh, never mind,	
Just a noise	ANTHONY
Just another noise,	You mustn't mind,
Something in the street,	It's a noise,
I'm a silly little	Just another noise,
Ninnynoddle—	Something in the street,
	You silly—

BOTH
(*Falling into each other's arms*)

Kiss me!

JOHANNA

Oh, sir . . .

ANTHONY

We'll go to Paris on Monday.

JOHANNA

What shall I wear?
I daren't pack!

ANTHONY
We'll ride a train . . .

JOHANNA
With you beside me on Sunday,
What will I care
What things I lack?

ANTHONY
Then sail to Spain . . .

JOHANNA	
I'll take my reticule.	
I need my reticule.	ANTHONY
You mustn't think	Why take your reticule?
Me a fool	We'll buy a reticule.
But my reticule	I'd never think
Never leaves my side,	You a fool,
It's the only thing	But a reticule—
My mother gave me—	Leave it all aside
Kiss me!	And begin again and
Kiss me!	Kiss me!
	I know a place where we can go
We'll go there,	Tonight.
Kiss me!	Kiss me!
We have a place where we can	We have a place where we can
Go . . .	Go tonight.

BEADLE
(*Simultaneously with the above*)
The name is Todd.

JUDGE
Todd?

BEADLE

Todd. Sweeney Todd.

JUDGE

Todd . . .

BEADLE

Todd.

JOHANNA	ANTHONY
I loved you	I loved you
Even as I saw you,	Even as I saw you,
Even as it does not	Even as it did not
Matter that I still	Matter that I did
Don't know your name, sir,	Not know your name . . .
Even as I saw you,	
Even as it does not	Johanna . . .
Matter that I still	Johanna . . .
Don't know your name . . .	Johanna . . .

BEADLE
(*Simultaneously with above*)

Todd . . . Sweeney Todd.

JUDGE *and* BEADLE

Sweeney Todd.

ANTHONY
(*Speaks*)

Anthony . . .

JUDGE

Todd . . .

BEADLE

Todd . . .

JOHANNA

Anthony . . .

JUDGE

Todd, eh?

JOHANNA	ANTHONY
I'll marry Anthony Sunday,	You marry Anthony Sunday,
That's what I'll do,	That's what you'll do,
No matter what!	No matter what!
I knew you'd come for me one day,	I knew I'd come for you one day
Only afraid that you'd forgot.	Only afraid that you'd forgot.

BEADLE
(*Simultaneously with above*)
Ladies in their sensitivities, my lord . . .

JUDGE

Pray lead the way.

BEADLE

Have a fragile sensibility . . .

JUDGE

Just as you say.

JOHANNA	ANTHONY
I feared you'd never come,	Marry me, marry me, miss,
That you'd been called away,	You'll marry me Sunday.
That you'd been killed,	Favor me, favor me
Had the plague,	With your hand.
Were in debtor's jail,	Promise,
Trampled by a horse,	Marry me, marry me,
Gone to sea again,	That you'll marry me—
Arrested by the . . .	Enough of all this . . .

(*He crushes her to him; they kiss*)

BEADLE
(*Simultaneously with above*)

When a girl's emergent,
Probably it's urgent . . .
Ladies in their sensitivities . . .

JUDGE

Todd . . .

JOHANNA
(*As she sinks to the floor with* ANTHONY)

Oh sir . . .

ANTHONY

Ah, miss . . .

JOHANNA
Oh, sir . . .
Oh, sir . . .
Oh, sir . . .
Oh, sir . . .
Oh, sir . . .
Oh, sir . . .

ANTHONY
Ah, miss . . .
Ah, miss . . .
Ah, miss . . .
Ah, miss . . .
Ah, miss . . .
Ah, miss . . .

(*Light leaves them, comes up on the pieshop-
tonsorial parlor. Upstairs,* TODD *is silently
cleaning his razor. In the shop,* MRS. LOVETT *and*
TOBIAS *unfreeze from the position in which they
were last seen*)

MRS. LOVETT

Maybe you should run along, dear.

TOBIAS

Oh no, ma'am, I daren't budge till he calls for me.

MRS. LOVETT

I'll pop up and see what Mr. Todd says.
> (*Humming,* MRS. LOVETT *starts climbing the stairs. As she enters the parlor*)

Ah me, me poor knees is not what they was, dear.
> (*She sits down on the chest*)

How long before the Eyetalian gets back?

TODD

> (*Still impassively cleaning the razor*)

He won't be back.

MRS. LOVETT

> (*Instantly suspicious*)

Now, Mr. T., you didn't!
> (TODD *nods toward the chest. Realizing,* MRS. LOVETT *jumps up. For a moment she stands looking at the chest, then, gingerly, she lifts the lid. She gazes down, then spins to* TODD)

You're crazy mad! Killing a man wot done you no harm? And the boy downstairs?

TODD

He recognized me from the old days. He tried to blackmail me, half my earnings forever.

MRS. LOVETT

Oh well, that's a different matter! What a relief, dear! For a moment I thought you'd lost your marbles.
> (*Turns to peer down again into the chest*)

Ooh! All that blood! Enough to make you come all over gooseflesh, ain't it. Poor bugger. Oh, well!
> (*She starts to close the lid, sees something, bends to pick it up. It is* PIRELLI'*s purse. She looks in it*)

Three quid! Well, waste not, want not, as I always say.
  (*She takes out the money and puts it down her
  bosom. She is about to throw the purse away
  when something about it attracts her. She slips
  it too down her dress. She shuts the chest lid
  and, quite composed again, sits down on it*)
Now, dear, we got to use the old noggin.
  (*As she sits deep in thought, we see the* JUDGE
  and BEADLE *coming up the street*)

BEADLE
(*Pointing*)
There you are, sir. Above the pieshop, sir.

JUDGE
I see. You may leave me now.

BEADLE
Thank you, sir. Thank you.
  (*He starts off as the* JUDGE *approaches the parlor*)

MRS. LOVETT
(*Coming out of her pondering*)
Well, first there's the lad.

TODD
Send him up here.

MRS. LOVETT
Him, too! Now surely one's enough for today, dear.
Shouldn't indulge yourself, you know. Now let me see,
he's half seas over already with the gin . . .

(As *she speaks, downstairs the* JUDGE *clangs the bell.* TODD *runs to the landing and peers down the stairs. The* BEADLE *is still visible, exiting*)

TODD

Providence is kind!

MRS. LOVETT

Who is it?

TODD

Judge Turpin.

MRS. LOVETT
(*Flustered*)

Him, him? The Judge? It can't be! It—

TODD

Quick, leave me!

MRS. LOVETT

What are you going to do?

TODD
(*Roaring*)

Leave me, I said!

MRS. LOVETT

Don't worry, dear. I'm—out!
(*She scuttles out of the tonsorial parlor and starts down the stairs as the* JUDGE *ascends. They meet halfway. She give him a deep curtsy*)
Excuse me, your Lordship.
(*She hurries back to* TOBIAS *in the shop*)

JUDGE

Mr. Todd?

TODD

At your service, sir. An honor to receive your patronage, sir.

MRS. LOVETT
(*To* TOBIAS)

Now, dear, seems like your guvnor has gone and left you high and dry. But don't worry. Your Aunt Nellie will think of what to do with you.
      (*Picks up the bottle of gin and pours some more
      into his glass. Still holding the bottle, she leads
      him toward the curtains*)
Come on into my lovely back parlor.
      (*They disappear through the curtains*)

JUDGE
(*Looking around*)

These premises are hardly prepossessing and yet the Beadle tells me you are the most accomplished of all the barbers in the city.

TODD

That is gracious of him, sir. And you must please excuse the modesty of my establishment. It's only a few days ago that I set up quarters here and some necessaries are yet to come.
      (*Indicating chair*)
Sit, sir, if you please, sir. Sit.
      (*The* JUDGE *settles into the chair; music under as*
      MRS. LOVETT, *still holding the gin bottle, enters
      her back parlor with* TOBIAS)

MRS. LOVETT

See how nice and cozy it is? Sit down, dear, sit.
(*She starts to pour him more gin*)
Oh, it's empty. Now you just sit there, dear, like a good
quiet boy while I get a new bottle from the larder.
(*She leaves him alone*)

TODD

And what may I do for you, sir? A stylish trimming of the
hair? A soothing skin massage?

JUDGE
(*Sings*)

You see, sir, a man infatuate with love,
Her ardent and eager slave.
So fetch the pomade and pumice stone
And lend me a more seductive tone,
A sprinkling perhaps of French cologne,
But first, sir, I think—a shave.

TODD

The closest I ever gave.
(*He whips the sheet over the* JUDGE, *then tucks
the bib in. The* JUDGE *hums, flicking imaginary
dust off the sheet;* TODD *whistles gaily*)

JUDGE
(*Speaks*)

You are in a merry mood today, Mr. Todd.

TODD
(*Sings, mixing lather*)

'Tis your delight, sir, catching fire
From one man to the next.

The Prologue's front drop depicting in a honeycomb
the class system of mid-19th Century England.

Mrs. Lovett (Angela Lansbury, *left*) confesses that hers are "The Worst Pies in London" and (*below*) recounts to Sweeney Todd (Len Cariou) the fate of his wife in the song "Poor Thing."

Once more in possession of his razors ("My Friends"), Todd promises that they will ". . . soon drip precious rubies."

Johanna (Sarah Rice) sings of her isolation in "Green Finch and Linnet Bird."

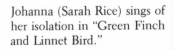

Martha Swope

On their first meeting (*above*) Anthony (Victor Garber) is instantly captivated by Johanna and (*left*) sings of his love ("Johanna") and determination to steal her away from her guardian.

Tobias (Ken Jennings) attempts to sell the crowd on the restorative powers of "Pirelli's Miracle Elixir."

"The Contest." Mrs. Lovett, Todd, customer (Frank Kopyc, *seated*), Pirelli (Joaquin Romaguera, *above center*), customer (Duane Bodin, *seated*) and Tobias.

Van Williams

In the song "Wait," Mrs. Lovett tries to calm Todd's growing impatience for vengeance by explaining that "Half the fun is to/Plan the plan."

Johanna and Anthony plan their escape in the duet "Kiss Me."

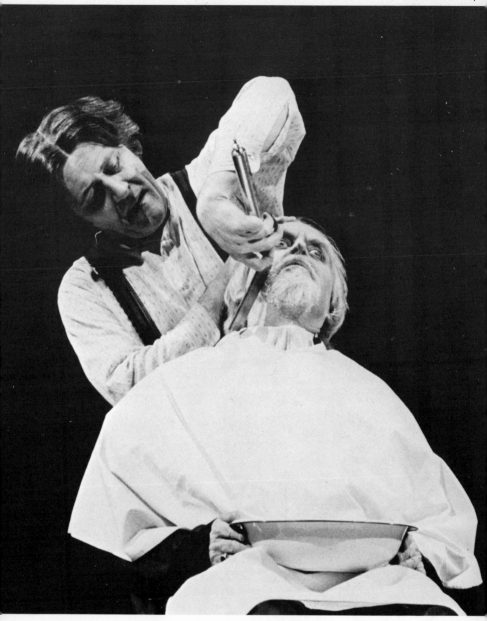

"Pretty Women," agree Todd and the Judge (Edmund Lyndeck), "How they make a man sing!"

"I will have revenge/I will have salvation!" soliloquizes
Todd in "Epiphany."

In the finale to Act I, Mrs. Lovett persuades Todd to accept her practical plan for disposing of his victims ("A Little Priest").

The opening of Act II finds the partnership of Todd and Mrs. Lovett a success, with the latter's customers voicing their opinion of her wares in the song "God, That's Good!"

Unknown to Anthony, Johanna has been locked away in Fogg's Asylum, and as he searches London for her, reprising "Johanna," Todd sings his version of the song (*overleaf*).

Mrs. Lovett sings of what it might be like living with Todd "By the Sea."

"Nothing's gonna harm you,"
Tobias promises Mrs. Lovett,
"Not While I'm Around."

Todd finally has his revenge.

In the Final Sequence, Todd holds the body of the dead Beggar Woman (Merle Louise) as a now demented Tobias avenges Todd's victims.

JUDGE

'Tis true, sir, love can still inspire
The blood to pound, the heart leap higher.

BOTH

What more, what more can man require—

JUDGE

Than love, sir?

TODD

More than love, sir.

JUDGE

What, sir?

TODD

Women.

JUDGE

Ah yes, women.

TODD

Pretty women.
   (*The* JUDGE *hums jauntily;* TODD *whistles and
   starts stropping his razor rhythmically. He then
   lathers the* JUDGE's *face. Still whistling, he
   stands back to survey the* JUDGE, *who is now
   totally relaxed, eyes closed. He picks up the razor
   and sings to it*)
Now then, my friend.
Now to your purpose.
Patience, enjoy it.
Revenge can't be taken in haste.

JUDGE
(*Opens his eyes*)
Make haste, and if we wed,
You'll be commended, sir.

TODD
(*Bows*)
My lord . . .
(*Goes to him*)
And who, may it be said,
Is your intended, sir?

JUDGE
My ward.
(TODD *freezes; the* JUDGE *closes his eyes, settles comfortably, speaks*)
And pretty as a rosebud.

TODD
(*Music rising*)
As pretty as her mother?

JUDGE
(*Mildly puzzled*)
What? What was that?
(As *the music reaches a shrill crescendo,* TODD *is slowly bringing the razor toward the* JUDGE'S *throat when suddenly the* JUDGE *opens his eyes and starts to twist around in curiosity*)

TODD
(*Musingly, lightly*)
Oh, nothing, sir. Nothing. May we proceed?
(*Starts to shave the* JUDGE, *sings*)

Pretty women . . .
Fascinating . . .
Sipping coffee,
Dancing . . .
Pretty women
Are a wonder.
Pretty women.

Sitting in the window or
Standing on the stair,
Something in them
Cheers the air.

Pretty women . . .

JUDGE

Silhouetted . . .

TODD

Stay within you . . .

JUDGE

Glancing . . .

TODD

Stay forever . . .

JUDGE

Breathing lightly . . .

TODD

Pretty women . . .

BOTH

Pretty women!
Blowing out their candles or
Combing out their hair . . .

JUDGE

Then they leave . . .

TODD

Even when they leave you   Even when they leave,
And vanish, they somehow   They still
Can still remain   Are
There with you,   There.
There with you.   They're there.

BOTH

Ah,
Pretty women . . .

TODD

At their mirrors . . .

JUDGE

In their gardens . . .

TODD

Letter-writing . . .

JUDGE

Flower-picking . . .

TODD

Weather-watching . . .

BOTH
How they make a man sing!
Proof of heaven
As you're living—
Pretty women, sir!

JUDGE
Pretty women, yes!
Pretty women, sir!
Pretty women!
Pretty women, sir!

TODD
Pretty women, here's to
Pretty women, all the
Pretty women . . .

(TODD *raises his arm in a huge arc and is about to slice the razor across the* JUDGE's *throat when* ANTHONY *bursts in*)

ANTHONY
(*Singing*)
She says she'll marry me Sunday,
Everything's set, we leave tonight—!

JUDGE
(*Jumping up, spilling the basin and knocking the razor from* TODD's *hand*)
You!

ANTHONY
Judge Turpin!

JUDGE
There is indeed a Higher Power to warn me thus in time.
(As ANTHONY *retreats, he jumps on him and grabs him by the arm*)
Johanna elope with you? Deceiving slut—I'll lock her up

in some obscure retreat where neither you nor any other vile, corrupting youth shall ever lay eyes on her again.

ANTHONY
(*Shaking himself free*)
But, sir, I beg of you—

JUDGE
(*To* TODD)
And as for you, barber, it is all too clear what company you keep. Service them well and hold their custom—for you'll have none of mine.
(*He strides out and down the stairs*)

ANTHONY
Mr. Todd!

TODD
(*Shouting*)
Out! Out, I say!
(*Bewildered,* ANTHONY *leaves. Music begins under, very agitated.* TODD *stands motionless, in shock. As the* JUDGE *hurries off down the street,* MRS. LOVETT, *with a new bottle of gin in her hand, sees him. She glances after him, then goes into the back parlor where* TOBIAS *is now asleep. She looks at him, puts down the bottle and hurries out and up the stairs to* TODD)

MRS. LOVETT
All this running and shouting. What is it now, dear?

TODD
I had him—and then . . .

MRS. LOVETT

The sailor busted in. I saw them both running down the street and I said to myself: "The fat's in the fire, for sure!"

TODD
(*Interrupting, sings*)

I had him!
His throat was bare
Beneath my hand—!

MRS. LOVETT
(*Alarmed, pacifying*)

There, there, dear. Don't fret.

TODD

No, I had him!
His throat was there,
And he'll never come again!

MRS. LOVETT

Easy now.
Hush, love, hush.
I keep telling you—

TODD
(*Violently*)

When?

MRS. LOVETT

What's your rush?

TODD

Why did I wait?
You told me to wait!

Now he'll never come again!
   (*Music becomes ferocious.* TODD's *insanity, al-*
  ways close to the surface, explodes finally)
There's a hole in the world
Like a great black pit
And it's filled with people
Who are filled with shit
And the vermin of the world
Inhabit it—
But not for long!

They all deserve to die!
Tell you why, Mrs. Lovett,
Tell you why:
Because in all of the whole human race, Mrs. Lovett,
There are two kinds of men and only two.
There's the one staying put
In his proper place
And the one with his foot
In the other one's face—
Look at me, Mrs. Lovett,
Look at you!

No, we all deserve to die!
Tell you why, Mrs. Lovett,
Tell you why:
Because the lives of the wicked should be—
              (*Slashes at the air*)
Made brief.
For the rest of us, death
Will be a relief—
We all deserve to die!
              (*Keening*)
And I'll never see Johanna,

No, I'll never hug my girl to me—
Finished!
           (*Turns on the audience*)
All right! You, sir,
How about a shave?
                (*Slashes twice*)
Come and visit
Your good friend Sweeney—!
You, sir, too, sir—
Welcome to the grave!
I will have vengeance,
I will have salvation!

Who, sir? You, sir?
No one's in the chair—
Come on, come on,
Sweeney's waiting!
I want you bleeders!
You, sir—anybody!
Gentlemen, now don't be shy!
Not one man, no,
Nor ten men,
Nor a hundred
Can assuage me—
I will have you!
              (*To* MRS. LOVETT)
And I *will* get him back
Even as he gloats.
In the meantime I'll practice
On less honorable throats.
              (*Keening again*)
And my Lucy lies in ashes
And I'll never see my girl again,
But the work waits,

I'm alive at last
> (*Exalted*)

And I'm full of joy!
> (*He drops down into the barber's chair in a sweat, panting*)

MRS. LOVETT
> (*Who has been watching him intently*)

That's all very well, but all that matters now is him!
> (*She points to the chest.* TODD *still sits motionless. She goes to him, peers at him*)

Listen! Do you hear me? Can you hear me? Get control of yourself.
> (*She slaps his cheek. After a long pause* TODD, *still in a half-dream, gets to his feet*)

What are we going to do about him? And there's the lad downstairs. We'd better go and have a look and be sure he's still there. When I left him he was sound asleep in the parlor.
> (*She starts downstairs*)

Come on!
> (TODD *follows. She disappears into the back parlor and re-emerges*)

No problem there. He's still sleeping. He's simple as a baby lamb. Later I can fob him off with some story easy. But him!
> (*Indicating the tonsorial parlor above*)

What are we going to do with him?

TODD
> (*Disinterestedly*)

Later on, when it's dark, we'll take him to some secret place and bury him.

MRS. LOVETT

Well, of course, we could do that. I don't suppose there's
any relatives going to come poking around looking for
him. But . . .

(*Pause. Chord*)

You know me. Sometimes ideas just pop into me head
and I keep thinking . . .

(*Sings*)

Seems a downright shame . . .

TODD

Shame?

MRS. LOVETT

Seems an awful waste . . .
Such a nice plump frame
Wot's-his-name
Has . . .
Had . . .
Has . . .
Nor it can't be traced.
Business needs a lift—
Debts to be erased—
Think of it as thrift,
As a gift . . .
If you get my drift . . .

(TODD *stares into space*)

No?

(*She sighs*)

Seems an awful waste.
I mean,
With the price of meat what it is,
When you get it,
If you get it—

TODD
(*Becoming aware*)

Ah!

MRS. LOVETT

Good, you got it.
(*Warming to it*)
Take, for instance,
Mrs. Mooney and her pie shop.
Business never better, using only
Pussycats and toast.
And a pussy's good for maybe six or
Seven at the most.
And I'm sure they can't compare
As far as taste—

TODD

Mrs. Lovett,
What a charming notion,   MRS. LOVETT
Eminently practical and yet   Well, it does seem a
Appropriate, as always.   Waste . . .
Mrs. Lovett
How I've lived without you   It's an idea . . .
All these years I'll never know! Think about it . . .
How delectable!   Lots of other gentlemen'll
Also undetectable.   Soon be coming for a shave
                                  Won't they?
                                  Think of
How choice!   All them
How rare!   Pies!

TODD
For what's the sound of the world out there?

MRS. LOVETT

What, Mr. Todd,
What, Mr. Todd,
What is that sound?

TODD

Those crunching noises pervading the air?

MRS. LOVETT

Yes, Mr. Todd,
Yes, Mr. Todd,
Yes, all around—

TODD

It's man devouring man, my dear,
And who are we
To deny it in here?

MRS. LOVETT

Then who are we
To deny it in here?

TODD

These are desperate times, Mrs. Lovett, and desperate
measures are called for.
*(She goes to the counter and comes back with an
imaginary pie)*

MRS. LOVETT

Here we are, hot from the oven.
(She holds it out to him)

TODD

What is that?

MRS. LOVETT

It's priest.
Have a little priest.

TODD

Is it really good?

MRS. LOVETT

Sir, it's too good,
At least.
Then again, they don't commit sins of the flesh,
So it's pretty fresh.

TODD
(*Looking at it*)

Awful lot of fat.

MRS. LOVETT

Only where it sat.

TODD

Haven't you got poet
Or something like that?

MRS. LOVETT

No, you see the trouble with poet
Is, how do you know it's
Deceased?
Try the priest.

TODD
(*Tasting it*)

Heavenly.

(MRS. LOVETT *giggles*)

Not as hearty as bishop, perhaps, but not as bland as
curate, either.

MRS. LOVETT

And good for business—always leaves you wanting more.
Trouble is, we only get it in Sundays . . .

(TODD *chuckles.* MRS. LOVETT *presents another imaginary pie*)
Lawyer's rather nice.

TODD

If it's for a price.

MRS. LOVETT

Order something else, though, to follow,
Since no one should swallow
It twice.

TODD

Anything that's lean.

MRS. LOVETT

Well, then, if you're British and loyal,
You might enjoy Royal
Marine.
                    (TODD *makes a face*)
Anyway, it's clean.
Though, of course, it tastes of wherever it's been.

TODD

                    (*Looking past her at an imaginary oven*)
Is that squire
On the fire?

MRS. LOVETT

Mercy no, sir,
Look closer,
You'll notice it's grocer.

TODD

Looks thicker.
More like vicar.

MRS. LOVETT

No, it has to be grocer—it's green.

TODD

The history of the world, my love—

MRS. LOVETT

Save a lot of graves,
Do a lot of relatives favors . . .

TODD

—is those below serving those up above.

MRS. LOVETT

Everybody shaves,
So there should be plenty of flavors . . .

TODD

How gratifying for once to know—

BOTH

—that those above will serve those down below!

MRS. LOVETT

Now, let's see . . .
    (Surveying an imaginary tray of pies on the
    counter)
We've got tinker . . .

                    TODD
              (*Looking at it*)
Something pinker.

                    MRS. LOVETT
Tailor?

                    TODD
              (*Shaking his head*)
Paler.

                    MRS. LOVETT
Butler?

                    TODD
Subtler.

                    MRS. LOVETT
Potter?

                    TODD
              (*Feeling it*)
Hotter.

                    MRS. LOVETT
Locksmith?
    (TODD *shrugs, defeated.* MRS. LOVETT *offers
    another imaginary pie*)
Lovely bit of clerk.

                    TODD
Maybe for a lark . . .

MRS. LOVETT
Then again, there's sweep
If you want it cheap
And you like it dark.
                    (*Another*)
Try the financier.
Peak of his career.

TODD
That looks pretty rank.

MRS. LOVETT
Well, he drank.
It's a bank
Cashier.
Last one really sold.
                    (*Feels it*)
Wasn't quite so old.

TODD
Have you any Beadle?

MRS. LOVETT
Next week, so I'm told.
Beadle isn't bad till you smell it
And notice how well it's
Been greased.
Stick to priest.
                    (*Offers another pie*)
Now this may be a bit stringy, but then, of course, it's
fiddle player.

TODD
This isn't fiddle player. It's piccolo player.

MRS. LOVETT

How can you tell?

TODD

It's piping hot.

(*Giggles*)

MRS. LOVETT
(*Snorts with glee*)
Then blow on it first.
(*He guffaws*)

TODD

The history of the world, my sweet—

MRS. LOVETT

Oh, Mr. Todd,
Ooh, Mr. Todd,
What does it tell?

TODD

—is who gets eaten and who get to eat.

MRS. LOVETT

And, Mr. Todd,
Too, Mr. Todd,
Who gets to sell.

TODD

But fortunately, it's also clear—

TODD	MRS. LOVETT
That everybody	But everybody
Goes down well with beer.	Goes down well with beer.

MRS. LOVETT

Since marine doesn't appeal to you, how about rear admiral?

TODD

Too salty. I prefer general.

MRS. LOVETT

With or without his privates? "With" is extra.
(TODD *chortles*)

TODD

(*As* MRS. LOVETT *offers another pie*)
What is that?

MRS. LOVETT

It's fop.
Finest in the shop.
Or we have some shepherd's pie peppered
With actual shepherd
On top.
And I've just begun.
Here's the politician—so oily
It's served with a doily—
(TODD *makes a face*)
Have one.

TODD

Put it on a bun.
(*As she looks at him quizzically*)
Well, you never know if it's going to run.

MRS. LOVETT

Try the friar.
Fried, it's drier.

TODD

No, the clergy is really
Too coarse and too mealy.

MRS. LOVETT

Then actor—
That's compacter.

TODD

Yes, and always arrives overdone.
I'll come again when you
Have Judge on the menu . . .

MRS. LOVETT

Wait! True, we don't have Judge—yet—but would you
settle for the next best thing?

TODD

What's that?

MRS. LOVETT
            (Handing him a butcher's cleaver)
Executioner.
    (TODD *roars, and then, picking up her wooden
    rolling pin, hands it to her)*

TODD

Have charity toward the world, my pet—

MRS. LOVETT

Yes, yes, I know, my love—

TODD

We'll take the customers that we can get.

MRS. LOVETT

High-born and low, my love.

TODD

We'll not discriminate great from small.
No, we'll serve anyone—
Meaning anyone—

BOTH

And to anyone
At all!

(*Music continues as the two of them brandish
their "weapons." The scene blacks out*)

ACT II

Thanks to her increasing prosperity, MRS.
LOVETT *has created a modest outdoor eating
garden outside the pieshop, consisting of a large
wooden table with two benches, a few bushes in
pots, birds in cages. At rise, contented customers, one of whom is drunk, are filling the garden,
devouring their pies and drinking ale while*
TOBIAS, *in a waiter's apron, drums up trade
along the sidewalk. Inside the pieshop,* MRS.
LOVETT, *in a "fancy" gown, a sign of her upward
mobility, doles out pies from the counter and
collects a few on a tray to bring into the garden
subsequently.* TODD *is pacing restlessly in the
tonsorial parlor. The* BEGGAR WOMAN *hangs
around throughout, hungry and ominous.*

TOBIAS

Ladies and gentlemen,
May I have your attention, perlease?
Are your nostrils aquiver and tingling as well
At that delicate, luscious ambrosial smell?
Yes they are, I can tell.

Well, ladies and gentlemen,
That aroma enriching the breeze
Is like nothing compared to its succulent source,
As the gourmets among you will tell you, of course.

Ladies and gentlemen,
You can't imagine the rapture in store—
                    (*Indicating the shop*)
Just inside of this door!
                    (*Beating his usual drum*)
There you'll sample
Mrs. Lovett's meat pies,
Savory and sweet pies,
As you'll see.
You who eat pies,
Mrs. Lovett's meat pies
Conjure up the treat pies
Used to be!

TOBIAS *and* CUSTOMERS
(*Sing simultaneously*)

1ST MAN:	Over here, boy, how about some ale?
2ND MAN:	Let me have another, laddie!
1ST WOMAN:	Tell me, are they flavorsome?
2ND WOMAN:	They are.
3RD WOMAN:	Isn't this delicious?
TOBIAS:	(*To 2ND MAN*) Right away.
4TH MAN:	Could we have some service over here, boy?
4TH WOMAN:	Could we have some service, waiter?
3RD MAN:	Could we have some service?
2ND *and* 3RD WOMEN:	Yes, they are.
1ST MAN:	God, that's good!

2ND MAN:	What about that pie, boy?
1ST WOMAN:	Tell me, are they spicy?
2ND WOMAN:	God, that's good!
5TH WOMAN:	How much are you charging?
TOBIAS:	Thruppence.
3RD WOMAN:	Yes, what about the pie, boy?
4TH WOMAN:	I never tasted anything so . . .
1ST and 5TH WOMEN:	Thruppence?
5TH MAN:	Thruppence for a meat pie?
1ST and 2ND MEN:	Where's the ale I asked you for, boy?
TOBIAS:	Ladies and gentlemen—!

MRS. LOVETT
(*Ringing a bell to attract* TOBIAS*'s attention*)
Toby!
(*She starts into the garden with a tray of pies*)

TOBIAS

Coming!
(*To a customer*)
'Scuse me . . .

MRS. LOVETT
(*Indicating a beckoning customer*)
Ale there!

TOBIAS
Right, mum!
(*He runs inside, picks up a jug of ale, whisks back out into the garden and starts filling tankards*)

MRS. LOVETT

Quick, now!

CUSTOMERS
(*Licking their fingers*)

God, that's good!

MRS. LOVETT

(A *bundle of activity, serving pies, collecting money, giving orders, addressing each of the patrons individually and with equal insincerity*)
Nice to see you, dearie . . .
How have you been keeping? . . .
Cor, me bones is weary!
Toby—!
(*Indicating a customer*)
One for the gentleman . . .
Hear the birdies cheeping—
Helps to keep it cheery . . .
(*Spying the* BEGGAR WOMAN)
Toby!
Throw the old woman out!

CUSTOMERS

God, that's good!
(TOBIAS *shoos the* BEGGAR WOMAN *away, but she soon comes back, sniffing*)

MRS. LOVETT

(*To other customers, without breaking rhythm*)
What's your pleasure, dearie? . . .
No, we don't cut slices . . .
Cor, me eyes is bleary! . . .

(As TOBIAS *is about to pour for a plastered cus-*
tomer)
Toby!
None for the gentleman! . . .
I could up me prices—
I'm a little leery . . .
Business
Couldn't be better, though—

CUSTOMERS

God, that's good!

MRS. LOVETT

Knock on wood.
                    (*She does*)

TODD
(*Leaning out of the window*)

Psst!

MRS. LOVETT
(*To a customer*)

Excuse me . . .

TODD

Psst!

MRS. LOVETT
(*To* TOBIAS)

Dear, see to the customers.

TODD

Psst!

MRS. LOVETT
(*Moving toward him*)
Yes, what, love?
Quick, though, the trade is brisk.

TODD

But it's six o'clock!

MRS. LOVETT

So it's six o'clock.

TODD

It was due to arrive
At a quarter to five—

TODD	MRS. LOVETT
And it's six o'clock!	And it's probably already Down the block!
I've been waiting all day!	It'll be here, it'll be here! Have a beaker of beer
But it should have been here By now!	And stop worrying, dear. Now, now . . .

CUSTOMERS

More hot pies!

MRS. LOVETT
(*Looking back, agitated at being pulled in two directions*)
Gawd.

(To TODD, *moving back to the garden)*

Will you wait there,	TODD
Coolly,	You'll come back
'Cos my customers truly	When it comes?
Are getting unruly.	

MRS. LOVETT
(Circulating again in the garden)
And what's your pleasure, dearie?
(Spilling ale)
Oops! I beg your pardon!
Just me hands is smeary—
(Spotting a would-be freeloader)
Toby!
Run for the gentleman!
(TOBIAS *catches him, collects the money;* MRS.
LOVETT *turns to another customer)*
Don't you love a garden?
Always makes me teary . . .
(Looking back at the freeloader)
Must be one of them foreigners—

CUSTOMERS
God that's good that is delicious!
*(During the following a huge crate appears high
on a crane and moves slowly downstage to the
tonsorial parlor.* TODD *sees it)*

MRS. LOVETT
What's my secret?
(To a woman)
Frankly, dear—forgive my candor—
Family secret,

All to do with herbs.
Things like being
Careful with your coriander,
That's what makes the gravy grander—!

CUSTOMERS

More hot pies!
(MRS. LOVETT *hastens into the shop and loads
the tray again*)
More hot!
More pies!

TODD
(*Out the window*)

Psst!

MRS. LOVETT
(*To a customer in the shop*)

Excuse me . . .

TODD

Psst!

MRS. LOVETT
(*To* TOBIAS)

Dear, see to the customers.

TODD

Psst!

MRS. LOVETT

Yes, what, love?
Quick, though, the trade is brisk.

TODD

But it's here!

MRS. LOVETT

It's where?

TODD

Coming up the stair!

MRS. LOVETT
(*Holding up the tray*)
I'll get rid of this lot
As they're still pretty hot

TODD

And then I'll be there!　It's about to be opened
Or don't you care?

No, I'll *be* there!
I will *be* there!　But we have to prepare!
But they'll never be sold
If I let 'em get cold—
(*During the following, the crate is lowered to the tonsorial parlor*)

MRS. LOVETT
(*Without pausing for breath, smiling to a customer*)
Oh, and
Incidentally, dearie,
You know Mrs. Mooney.
Sales 've been so dreary—
(*Spots the* BEGGAR WOMAN *again*)
Toby—!
(*To the same customer*)
Poor thing is penniless.
(*Indicating* BEGGAR WOMAN, *to* TOBIAS)
What about that loony?
(*To the same customer, as* TOBIAS *shoos the* BEGGAR WOMAN *away again*)

Lookin' sort of beery—
Oh well, got her comeuppance—
 (*Hawklike, to a rising customer*)
And that'll be thruppence—and

CUSTOMERS
(*Singing with mouths full*)   MRS. LOVETT
God, that's good that is de have you   So she should.
Licious ever tasted smell such
Oh my God what more that's pies good!
 (MRS. LOVETT *goes up to the tonsorial parlor,*
 entering as TODD *opens the crate, revealing an*
 elaborate barber chair)

TODD *and* MRS. LOVETT
(*Swooning with admiration*)
Oooohhhh! Oooohhhh!
 (*The empty crate swings away on the crane*)

TODD
Is that a chair fit for a king,   MRS. LOVETT
A wondrous neat   It's gorgeous!
And most particular chair?   It's gorgeous!
You tell me where
Is there a seat
Can half compare   It's perfect!
With this particular thing!   It's gorgeous!
I have a few
Minor adjustments   You make your few
To make—   Minor adjustments.
They'll take
A moment.   You take your time,
I'll call you . . .   I'll go see to the customers.

TODD

(*Looking at the chair, as* MRS. LOVETT *goes back to the garden*)

I have another friend . . .

TOBIAS

(*To the customers*)

Is that a pie fit for a king,	MRS. LOVETT
A wondrous sweet	It's gorgeous!
And most delectable thing?	It's gorgeous!
You see, ma'am, why	
There is no meat	
Pie can compete	It's perfect!
With this delectable	It's gorgeous!
Pie.	

CUSTOMERS

(*Simultaneously with above*)

Yum!
Yum!
Yum!

TOBIAS *and* MRS. LOVETT

The crust all velvety and wavy,
That glaze, those crimps . . .
And then the thick, succulent gravy . . .
One whiff, one glimpse . . .

CUSTOMERS

(*Simultaneously with above*)

Yum! Yum!
Yum! Yum!
Yum! Yum!
Yum! Yum!

TODD

And now to test
This best of barber chairs . . .

MRS. LOVETT
So rich,   TOBIAS
So thick   So tender
It makes you sick . . . That you surrender . . .

CUSTOMERS
(*Simultaneously with above*)

Yum!
Yum!
Yum! Yum!

TODD

It's time . . .
It's time . . .
Psst!

MRS. LOVETT
(*To the customers*)

Excuse me . . .

TODD
(*From above*)

Psst!

MRS. LOVETT
(*To* TOBIAS)

Dear, see to the customers.

TODD

Psst!

MRS. LOVETT
(*Moving toward him*)
Yes, what, love?

TODD
Quick, now!

MRS. LOVETT
Me heart's aflutter—!

TODD	MRS. LOVETT
When I pound the floor,	When you pound the floor,
It's a signal to show	Yes, you told me, I know,
That I'm ready to go,	You'll be ready to go
When I pound the floor!	When you pound the floor—
	Will you trust me?
I just want to be sure.	Will you trust me?
	I'll be waiting below
When I'm certain that you're	For the whistle to blow . . .
In place—	

TODD
I'll pound three times.
    (*He demonstrates on the frame of the window*)
Three times.
        (*He does it again; she nods impatiently*)
And then you—
           (*She knocks at the air two times*)
Three times—
      (*She knocks heavily and wearily on the wall*)
If you—
        (*She knocks again, rolling her eyes skyward*)
Exactly.

CUSTOMERS

More hot pies!

MRS. LOVETT

Gawd!

CUSTOMERS

More hot!

MRS. LOVETT
(*Over her shoulder to them*)

Right!

CUSTOMERS

More pies!

TODD
(*Seeing her attention waver*)

Psst!

CUSTOMERS

More!

MRS. LOVETT

Wait!
(*She runs into the bakehouse, which we see for the first time. Upstage are the large baking ovens. Downstage is a butcher's-block table, on which stands a bizarre meat-grinding machine. In the wall is the mouth of a chute leading down from the tonsorial parlor. Upstage is a trap door leading down to an invisible cellar. While music continues under,* TODD *takes a stack of books tied together, puts it in the chair, then pounds*

three times on the floor. MRS. LOVETT *responds by knocking three times on the mouth of the chute.* TODD *pulls a lever in the arm of the chair. The books disappear through a trap. Music. The books reappear from the hole in the bakehouse wall and plop on the floor.* MRS. LOVETT *knocks three times excitedly on the chute;* TODD *responds by pounding on the floor three times*)

CUSTOMERS

More hot pies!
   (MRS. LOVETT *hurries out of the bakehouse*)
More hot! More pies!
   (TODD *resumes tinkering happily with the chair*)
More! Hot! Pies!

MRS. LOVETT *and* TOBIAS
(To the customers)

Eat them slow and
Feel the crust, how thin I (she) rolled it!
Eat them slow, 'cos
Every one's a prize!
Eat them slow, 'cos
That's the lot and now we've sold it!
   (*She hangs up a "Sold Out" sign*)
Come again tomorrow—!

MRS. LOVETT
(Spotting something along the street)

Hold it—

CUSTOMERS

More hot pies!

MRS. LOVETT

Bless my eyes—!
(For she sees the MAN WITH CAP, *from Act I,
approaching the barber sign. He looks up and
rings* TODD's *bell—three times)*
Fresh supplies!
*(*TODD *leans out, sees the man, beckons him up;
the man starts up the steps.* TODD *holds his
razor. They both freeze.* MRS.LOVETT *takes down
the "Sold Out" sign and turns back to the customers)*

MRS. LOVETT	TOBIAS
How about it, dearie?	Is that a pie
Be here in a twinkling!	Fit for a king,
Just confirms my theory—	A wondrous sweet
Toby—!	And most delectable
God watches over us.	Thing?
Didn't have an inkling . . .	You see, ma'am, why
Positively eerie . . .	There is no meat pie—

CUSTOMERS
(Simultaneously with above)

Yum!
Yum!
Yum!
Yum! Yum!
Yum!
Yum!

MRS. LOVETT
(Spotting the BEGGAR WOMAN *again)*
Toby!
Throw the old woman out!

(As TOBIAS *leads the* BEGGAR WOMAN *off again,*
MRS. LOVETT *runs back to the pieshop*)

CUSTOMERS
(*Starting with their mouths full, gradually swal-
lowing and singing clearly*)
God that's good that is de have you
Licious ever tasted smell such
Oh my God what perfect more that's
Pies such flavor
    (MRS. LOVETT *relaxes in the pieshop with a mug
    of ale*)
God that's good!!!

(*The scene blacks out. The chimes of St.
Dunstan's sound softly. It is dawn.* ANTHONY *is
searching the streets of London for* JOHANNA)

ANTHONY
I feel you, Johanna,
I feel you.
Do they think that walls can hide you?
Even now I'm at your window.
I am in the dark beside you,
Buried sweetly in your yellow hair,
Johanna . . .
    (*As he continues the search, the light comes up
    on the tonsorial parlor.* TODD *is seated on the
    outside stairs, smoking and enjoying the morn-
    ing. During the following passage, a customer
    arrives.* TODD *ushers him into the office and into
    the chair, preparing him for a shave. Throughout
    the song,* TODD *remains benign, wistful, dream-*

like. What he sings is totally detached from the
action, as is he. He sings to the air)

TODD

And are you beautiful and pale,
With yellow hair, like her?
I'd want you beautiful and pale,
The way I've dreamed you were,
Johanna . . .

ANTHONY

Johanna . . .

TODD

And if you're beautiful, what then,
With yellow hair, like wheat?
I think we shall not meet again—
        (He slashes the customer's throat)
My little dove, my sweet
Johanna . . .

ANTHONY

I'll steal you,
Johanna . . .

TODD

Goodbye, Johanna.
You're gone, and yet you're mine.
I'm fine, Johanna,
I'm fine!
    (He pulls the lever and the customer disap-
    pears down the chute)

ANTHONY
Johanna . . .
(*Night falls. We see a wisp of smoke rise from the
bakehouse chimney, a small trail gradually bel-
lowing out into a great, noxious plume of black.
As it thickens, we become aware of* MRS. LOVETT,
*in a white nightdress, inside the bakehouse. The
oven doors are open and cast a hot light. She is
tossing "objects" into the oven. As the music
continues under, a figure stumbles into view
from the alleyway beside the chimney. It is the*
BEGGAR WOMAN, *coughing and spitting and carrying a meager straw pallet, her bed*)

BEGGAR WOMAN
(*In a rage, loudly, sings*)
Smoke! Smoke!
Sign of the devil! Sign of the devil!
City on fire!
(*She tries to interest passers-by but, clearly
revolted by her, they move away*)
Witch! Witch!
(*Spits at the bakehouse*)
Smell it, sir! An evil smell!
Every night at the vespers bell—
Smoke that comes from the mouth of hell—
City on fire!
(*The smoke trails away as dawn comes up*)
City on fire . . .
Mischief! Mischief!
Mischief . . .
(*She shuffles off. It is now the next day.* AN-
THONY *is searching through another part of Lon-*

don. TODD *is upstairs and looking pleasantly
down at the street. A second customer arrives
and is shown into the shop and prepared, as before)*

TODD

And if I never hear your voice,
My turtledove, my dear,
I still have reason to rejoice:
The way ahead is clear,
Johanna . . .

JOHANNA'S VOICE

(Heard only by ANTHONY, *she becomes visible
behind bars in a section of the madhouse, Fogg's
Asylum, in which she is incarcerated)*
I'll marry Anthony Sunday . . .
Anthony Sunday . . .

ANTHONY

I feel you . . .

TODD

And in that darkness when I'm blind
With what I can't forget—

ANTHONY

Johanna . . .

TODD

It's always morning in my mind,
My little lamb, my pet,
Johanna . . .

JOHANNA'S VOICE
I knew you'd come for me one day . . .
Come for me . . . one day . . .

TODD   ANTHONY
You stay, Johanna—   Johanna . . .
   (*As they both sing the second syllable of the
name*, TODD *slashes the second customer's throat
so that his mouth opens simultaneously with
theirs*)

TODD
The way I've dreamed you are.
   (*Dusk gathers*; TODD *looks up*)
Oh look, Johanna—
   (*He pulls the lever and the customer disappears*)
A star!

ANTHONY
Buried sweetly in your yellow hair . . .

TODD
   (*Tossing the customer's hat down the chute*)
A shooting star!
   (*Night falls again. Smoke rises.* MRS. LOVETT *is
again in the bakehouse.* The BEGGAR WOMAN
reappears, coughing fit to kill)

BEGGAR WOMAN
   (*Pointing*)
There! There!
Somebody, somebody look up there!
   (*Passers-by continue to ignore her*)
Didn't I tell you? Smell that air!

City on fire!
Quick, sir! Run and tell!
Warn 'em all of the witch's spell!
There it is, there it is, the unholy smell!
Tell it to the Beadle and the police as well!
Tell 'em! Tell 'em!
Help!!! Fiend!!!
City on fire!!!

> (*The smoke thins; dawn rises*)

City on fire . . .
Mischief . . . Mischief . . . Mischief . . .
  (*She makes a feeble curse with her fingers at the
  bakehouse*)
Fiend . . .

> (*Shrugs, turns pathetically to a passer-by*)

Alms . . . alms . . .
  (*She shuffles off again. During the last section of
  the song, which follows,* TODD *welcomes a third
  customer. He does not kill this one because a
  wife and child are waiting outside—the child
  has entered the room and sits on the chest watching* TODD. *By the end of the song* TODD *is again
  looking softly up at the sky*)

TODD
(*Shaving the customer*)
And though I'll think of you, I guess,
Until the day I die,
I think I miss you less and less
As every day goes by,
Johanna . . .

ANTHONY
Johanna . . .

JOHANNA'S VOICE
With you beside me on Sunday,
Married on Sunday . . .

TODD
(Sadly)
And you'd be beautiful and pale,
And look too much like her.
If only angels could prevail,
We'd be the way we were,
Johanna . . .

ANTHONY
I feel you . . .
Johanna . . .

JOHANNA'S VOICE
Married on Sunday . . .
Married on Sunday . . .

TODD
(Cheerfully, looking up at the sky)
Wake up, Johanna!
Another bright red day!
                (Wistful smile)
We learn, Johanna,
To say
Goodbye . . .
    (Having completed the shave, TODD accepts
    money from the customer, who leaves with his
    family)

ANTHONY
(Disappearing into the distance)
I'll steal you . . .

(The scene fades and we see the barred door to Fogg's Asylum. From inside we hear a weird and frightening sound, the cries and jibbers of the inmates. After a moment, rising above the bizarre cacophony, we hear JOHANNA's *voice from inside a window, singing a snatch of "Green Finch and Linnet Bird." A few moments later, she breaks off singing and the inmates quieten too as* ANTHONY, *dejected, enters. As he starts across the stage, once again we hear* JOHANNA's *voice, singing)*

ANTHONY
(Incredulous, overjoyed, stops in his tracks)
Johanna!
(Calling excitedly up at a window)
Johanna! Johanna!
(A male passer-by enters)
Oh sir, please tell me. What house is this?

PASSER-BY
That? That's Mr. Fogg's Private Asylum for the Mentally Deranged.

ANTHONY
A madhouse!

PASSER-BY
I'd keep away from there if I were you.
(He exits. Once again we hear JOHANNA's *voice)*

ANTHONY
Johanna! Johanna!
(He starts beating wildly on the door)
Open! Open the door!

(*The* BEADLE, *falsely amiable as ever, swaggers
on, recognizes him*)

BEADLE
Now, now, friend, what's all this hollering and shouting?

ANTHONY
Oh, sir, there has been a monstrous perversion of justice. A young woman, as sane as you or I, has been incarcerated there.

BEADLE
Is that a fact? Now what is this young person's name?

ANTHONY
Johanna.

BEADLE
Johanna. That wouldn't by any chance be Judge Turpin's ward?

ANTHONY
He's the one. He's the devil incarnate who has done this to her.

BEADLE
You watch your tongue. That girl's as mad as the seven seas. I brought her here myself. So—hop it.

ANTHONY
You have no right to order me about.

BEADLE
No right, eh? You just hop it or I'm booking you for disturbing of the peace, assailing an officer—

ANTHONY

Is there no justice in this city? Are the officers of the law
as vicious and corrupted as their masters? Johanna!
Johanna!

> (*With a little what-can-you-do? shrug, the*
> BEADLE *blows a whistle. Two policemen hurry
> on. The* BEADLE *nods to* ANTHONY. *The police-
> men jump on him but just before they subdue
> him, he breaks loose and runs away. The police-
> men start after him*)

BEADLE
(*Calling after them*)

After him! Get him! Bash him on the head if need be!
That's the sort of scalawag that gets this neighborhood
into disrepute.

> (As *the scene dims we hear first, in the darkness,
> the shrieks and moans of the asylum inmates.
> Then loud and raucous, banishing them, we
> hear the sound of* MRS. LOVETT *singing, as lights
> come up on her back parlor*)

MRS. LOVETT
(*Sitting at a harmonium*)

I am a lass who alas loves a lad
Who alas has a lass
In Canterbury.
'Tis a row dow diddle dow day
'Tis a row dow diddle dow dee . . .

> (*The parlor has been prettied up with new
> wallpaper and a second-hand harmonium.* TODD
> *is sitting on the love seat, cleaning his pipe.*
> MRS. LOVETT *is using the harmonium as a desk.*

*She has a little cash book and is counting out
shillings and pennies in piles)*
Nothing like a nice sit down, is there, dear, after a hard
day's work?
(Piling up coins)
Four and thruppence . . . four and eleven pence . . .
(Makes a note in the book and does some adding)
That makes seven pounds nine shillings and four pence
for this week. Not bad—and that don't include wot I had
to pay out for my nice cheery wallpaper *or* the har-
monium . . .
(Patting it approvingly)
And a real bargain it was, dear, it being only partly singed
when the chapel burnt down.
(Glancing at the unresponsive TODD)
Mr. T., are you listening to me?

TODD

Of course.

MRS. LOVETT

Then what did I say, eh?

TODD
(Back in his reflections)
There *must* be a way to the Judge.

MRS. LOVETT
(Cross)
The bloody old Judge! Always harping on the bloody old
Judge!
(She massages his neck)
We got a nice respectable business now, money coming
in regular and—since we're careful to pick and

choose—only strangers and such like wot won't be missed—who's going to catch on?

> (*No response; she leans across and pecks him on the lips; music*)

Ooh, Mr. Todd—

> (*Kisses him again*)

I'm so happy—

> (*Again*)

I could—

> (*Again*)

Eat you up, I really could!
You know what I'd like to
Do, Mr. Todd?

> (*Kisses him*)

What I dream—

> (*Again*)

If the business stays as good,
Where I'd really like to go—

> (*No response*)

In a year or so . . .

> (*No response*)

Don't you want to know?

TODD
(*Dully*)

Of course.

MRS. LOVETT

Do you really want to know?

TODD
(*Feigned enthusiasm*)

Yes, yes, I do, I do.

> (*Music continues under*)

MRS. LOVETT
(*Settling back, after a pause*)
I've always had a dream—ever since I was a skinny little
slip of a thing and my rich Aunt Nettie used to take me to
the seaside August Bank Holiday . . . the pier . . .
making little castles in the sand. I can still feel me toes
wiggling around in the briny.
(*She sings*)
By the sea, Mr. Todd,
That's the life I covet;
By the sea, Mr. Todd,
Ooh, I know you'd love it!
You and me, Mr. T.,
We could be alone
In a house wot we'd almost own
Down by the sea . . .

TODD
Anything you say . . .

MRS. LOVETT
Wouldn't that be smashing?
(TODD *gives her a pained smile*)
With the sea at our gate,
We'll have kippered herring
Wot have swum to us straight
From the Straits of Bering.
Every night in the kip
When we're through our kippers,
I'll be there slippin' off your slippers
By the sea . . .
With the fishies splashing,
By the sea . . .

Wouldn't that be smashing?
Down by the sea—

TODD

Anything you say,
Anything you say.

MRS. LOVETT

I can see us waking,
The breakers breaking,
The seagulls squawking:
Hoo! Hoo!
   (*She thinks she's being charming;* TODD *looks at
   her in terror*)
I do me baking,
Then I go walking
With you-hoo . . .
                    (*Waves*)
Yoo-hoo . . .

I'll warm me bones
On the esplanade,
Have tea and scones
With me gay young blade,
Then I'll knit a sweater
While you write a letter,
                    (*Coyly*)
Unless we got better
To do-hoo . . .

TODD
(*Speaks*)

Anything you say . . .

MRS. LOVETT

Think how snug it'll be
Underneath our flannel
When it's just you and me
And the English Channel.
In our cozy retreat,
Kept all neat and tidy,
We'll have chums over every Friday
By the sea . . .

TODD

Anything you say . . .

MRS. LOVETT

Don't you love the weather
By the sea?
We'll grow old together
By the seaside,
Hoo! Hoo!
By the beautiful sea!
(*She speaks, music under*)
Oh, I can see us now—in our bathing dresses—you in a
nice rich navy—and me, stripes perhaps.
(*Sings*)
It'll be so quiet
That who'll come by it
Except a seagull?
Hoo! Hoo!
We shouldn't try it,
Though, till it's legal
For two-hoo!

But a seaside wedding
Could be devised,

Me rumpled bedding
Legitimized.
Me eyelids'll flutter,
I'll turn into butter,
The moment I mutter
"I do-hoo!"
      (TODD *gives her a rather appalled glance*)
By the sea, in our nest,
We could share our kippers
With the odd paying guest
From the weekend trippers,
Have a nice sunny suite
For the guest to rest in—
Now and then, you could do the guest in—
By the sea.
Married nice and proper,
By the sea—
Bring along your chopper
To the seaside,
           (*Two slashes*)
Hoo! Hoo!
By the beautiful sea!
(*Just before the end of the song, she plays a measure of "Here Comes the Bride" on the harmonium. After the song, she nuzzles up to* TODD *on the love seat*)
Come on, dear. Give us a kiss.
          (*Kisses him*)
Ooh, that was lovely. Now, Mr. T., you do love me just a little bit, don't you?

TODD

Of course.

MRS. LOVETT

Then how about it? Of course, there'd have to be a little visit to St. Swithin's to legalize things. But that wouldn't be too painful, would it?

TODD
(*Back with his obsession*)

I'll make them pay for what they did to Lucy.

MRS. LOVETT
(*Almost scolding*)

Now, dear, you listen to me. It's high time you forgot all them morbid fancies. Your Lucy's gone, poor thing. It's your Nellie now. Here.
(*She takes a bon-bon from her purse*)
Have a nice bon-bon.
(*She kisses him over the bon-bon, has a thought*)
You know, it's seventeen years this Whitsun since my poor Albert passed on. I don't see why I shouldn't be married in white, do you?
(*From the pieshop, upstage, we hear* ANTHONY *calling*)

ANTHONY
(*Off*)

Mr. Todd! Mr. Todd!
(*He comes running in*)
I've found her!

TODD
(*Jumping up*)

You have found Johanna?

ANTHONY

That monster of a Judge has had her locked away in a madhouse!

TODD

Where? Where?

ANTHONY

Where no one can reach her, at Mr. Fogg's Asylum. Oh, Mr. Todd, she's in there with those screeching, gibbering maniacs—

TODD

A madhouse! A madhouse!
  (*Swinging around, feverishly excited, buzzing
  music under*)
Johanna is as good as rescued.

MRS. LOVETT
  (*Bewildered*)

She is?

TODD

Where do you suppose all the wigmakers of London go to obtain their human hair?

MRS. LOVETT

Who knows, dear? The morgue, wouldn't be surprised.

TODD

Bedlam. They get their hair from the lunatics at Bedlam.

ANTHONY

Then you think—?

TODD

Fogg's Asylum? Why not? For the right amount, they will sell you the hair off any madman's head—

MRS. LOVETT

And the scalp to go with it too, if requested. Excuse me, gentlemen, I'm out!

(*Exits*)

TODD

(*Excitedly, to* ANTHONY)

We will write a letter to this Mr. Fogg offering the highest price for hair the exact shade of Johanna's—which I trust you know?

ANTHONY

Yellow.

TODD

Not exact enough. I must make you into a credible wigmaker—and quickly.

(*Sings*)

There's tawny and there's golden saffron,
There's flaxen and there's blonde . . .

(*Speaks*)

Repeat that. Repeat that!

ANTHONY

Yes, Mr. Todd.

TODD

Well?

ANTHONY

There's tawny and there's golden saffron,
There's flaxen and there's blonde . . .

144

TODD

Good.

(*Sings*)
There's coarse and fine,
There's straight and curly,   ANTHONY
There's gray, there's white,   There's coarse and fine,
There's ash, there's pearly,   There's straight and curly,
There's corn-yellow,   There's gray, there's white,
Buff and ochre and   There's ash, there's pearly,
Straw and apricot . . .   There's corn-yellow . . .

(*They exit. As the lights dim, a quintet from the
company appears*)

QUINTET
(*Variously*)
Sweeney'd waited too long before—
"Ah, but never again," he swore.
Fortune arrived. "Sweeney!" it sang.
Sweeney was ready, and Sweeney sprang.
Sweeney's problems went up in smoke,
All resolved with a single stroke.
Sweeney was sharp, Sweeney was burning,
Sweeney began the engines turning.
Sweeney's problems went up in smoke,
All resolved and completely solved
With a single stroke
By Sweeney!
Sweeney
Didn't wait,
Not Sweeney!
Set the bait,
Did Sweeney!
Sweeney! Sweeney! Sweeney!

(*During this,* TODD *appears on the staircase, ac-*

companied by a strange figure; they enter the tonsorial parlor. We soon realize the figure is AN-THONY, disguised as a wigmaker)

ANTHONY
(Finishing his catechism)
  With finer textures,
  Ash looks fairer,   TODD
  Which makes it rare,   Good.
  But flaxen's rarer—

                      No! No!
  Yes, yes, I know—   The flaxen's cheaper . . .
  Cheaper, not rarer . . .
        (Music continues under)

TODD
Here's money.
        (Hands him purse)
And here's the pistol.
        (Hands him a gun)
For kill if you must. Kill.

ANTHONY
I'll kill a dozen jailers if need be to set her free.

TODD
Then off with you, off. But, Anthony, listen to me once again. When you have rescued her, bring her back here. I shall guard her while you hire the chaise to Plymouth.

ANTHONY
We'll be with you before the evening's out,
     (Clasping both TODD's *hands)*
Mr. Todd. Oh, thank you—friend.

(*He hurries off.* TODD *goes to a little writing
table, picks up a quill pen and starts to write.
The quintet sings what he writes*)

QUINTET
(*Variously, as* TODD *writes*)
Most Honorable Judge Turpin—
(TODD *pauses reflectively*)
Most Honorable—
(TODD *snorts derisively*)
Honorable!
(*He resumes writing*)
I venture thus to write you this—
(*Thinks, choosing the word*)
Urgent note to warn you that the hot-blooded—
(*Thinks*)
Young—
(*Grunts with satisfaction*)
Sailor has abducted your ward Johanna—
(*Stares off sadly*)
Johanna—Johanna—
(*Resumes writing*)
From the institution where you—
(*Thinks*)
So wisely confined her but,
Hoping to earn your favor,
I have persuaded the boy to lodge her here tonight
At my tonsorial parlor—
(*Dips the pen*)
In Fleet Street.
If you want her again in your arms,
Hurry
After the night falls.

*(He starts to sign, then adds another phrase with
a smile)*
She will be waiting.

    (Reads it over)

Waiting . . .

    (Dips pen again, writing carefully)
Your obedient humble servant,
Sweeney

    (A flourish of the pen)

Todd.

(Music continues under as TODD *hurries across
the stage to* JUDGE TURPIN'S *house, knocks on the
door, which opens, and hands in the letter)*

TODD

Give this to Judge Turpin. It's urgent.

*(As he disappears, lights come up on the eating
garden. It is early evening. The garden is
deserted.* MRS. LOVETT *is sitting on the steps
knitting a half-finished muffler. The bells of St.
Dunstan's sound. After a beat,* TOBIAS *emerges
from the shop with a "Sold Out" sign, puts it on
the shop door, and goes to* MRS. LOVETT)

TOBIAS

I put the sold-out sign up, ma'am.

MRS. LOVETT

That's my boy.

    (Holding up the knitting)
Look, dear! A lovely muffler and guess who it's for.

TOBIAS

Coo, ma'am. For me?

MRS. LOVETT

Wouldn't you like to know!

TOBIAS

Oh, you're so good to me, ma'am. Sometimes, when I think what it was like with Signor Pirelli—it seems like the Good Lord sent you for me.

MRS. LOVETT

It's just my warm heart, dear. Room enough there for all God's creatures.

TOBIAS

(Coming closer, hovering, very earnest)

You know, ma'am, there's nothing I wouldn't do for you. If there was a monster or an ogre or anything bad like that wot was after you, I'd rip it apart with my bare fists, I would.

MRS. LOVETT

What a sweet child it is.

TOBIAS

Or even if it was just a man . . .

MRS. LOVETT

(Somewhat uneasy)

A man, dear?

TOBIAS

(Exaggeratedly conspiratorial)

A man wot was bad and wot might be luring you all unbeknownst into his evil deeds, like.

MRS. LOVETT
(*Even more wary*)
What is this? What are you talking about?

TOBIAS
(*Sings*)
Nothing's gonna harm you,
Not while I'm around.

MRS. LOVETT
Of course not, dear, and why should it?

TOBIAS
Nothing's gonna harm you,
No, sir,
Not while I'm around.

MRS. LOVETT
What do you mean, "a man"?

TOBIAS
Demons are prowling
Everywhere
Nowadays.

MRS. LOVETT
(*Somewhat relieved, patting his head*)
And so they are, dear.

TOBIAS
I'll send 'em howling,
I don't care—
I got ways.

MRS. LOVETT

Of course you do . . . What a sweet, affectionate child
it is.

TOBIAS

No one's gonna hurt you,
No one's gonna dare.

MRS. LOVETT

I know what Toby deserves. . .

TOBIAS

Others can desert you—
Not to worry—
Whistle, I'll be there.

MRS. LOVETT

Here, have a nice bong-bong.
    (*Starts to reach for her purse, but* TOBIAS *stays
her hand in adoration*)

TOBIAS

Demons 'll charm you
With a smile
For a while,
But in time
Nothing can harm you,
Not while I'm around.
    (*Music continues*)

MRS. LOVETT

What is this foolishness? What're you talking about?

TOBIAS

Little things wot I've been thinking and wondering
about. . . . It's him, you see—Mr. Todd. Oh, I know
you fancy him, but men ain't like women, they ain't wot
you can trust, as I've lived and learned.

(*She looks at him uneasily*)

Not to worry, not to worry,
I may not be smart but I ain't dumb.
I can do it,
Put me to it,
Show me something I can overcome.
Not to worry, mum.

Being close and being clever
Ain't like being true.
I don't need to, I won't never
Hide a thing from you,
Like some.

(*Music continues under*)

MRS. LOVETT

Now Toby dear, haven't we had enough foolish chatter?
Let's just sit nice and quiet for a bit. Here.

(*She pulls out the chatelaine purse, which is
now immediately recognizable to the audience
as* PIRELLI's *money purse, and starts to fumble in
it for a bon-bon*)

TOBIAS

(*Suddenly excited, pointing*)

That! That's Signor Pirelli's purse!

(MRS. LOVETT, *realizing her slip, quickly hides
it*)

MRS. LOVETT
(*Stalling for time*)
What's that? What was that, dear?

TOBIAS
That proves it! What I've been thinking. That's his purse.

MRS. LOVETT
(*Concealing what is now almost panic*)
Silly boy! It's just a silly little something Mr. T. gave me for my birthday.

TOBIAS
Mr. Todd gave it to you! And how did he get it? How did he get it?

MRS. LOVETT
Bought it, dear. In the pawnshop, dear.
(*To distract him, she lifts the unfinished muffler on its needles*)
Come on now.
(*Sings*)
Nothing's gonna harm you,
Not while I'm around!
Nothing's gonna harm you, Toby,
Not while I'm around.

TOBIAS
You don't understand.
(*Sings*)
Two quid was in it,
Two or three—
(*Speaks, music continuing*)

The guvnor giving up his purse—with two quid?
(*Sings*)
Not for a minute!
Don't you see?
(*Speaks, music under*)
It was in Mr. Todd's parlor that the guvnor disappeared.

MRS. LOVETT
(*With a weak laugh*)
Boys and their fancies! What will we think of next! Here,
dear. Sit here by your Aunt Nellie like a good boy and
look at your lovely muffler. How warm it's going to keep
you when the days draw in. And it's so becoming on you.

TOBIAS
(*Sings*)
Demons 'll charm you
With a smile
For a while,
But in time
Nothing's gonna harm you,
Not while I'm around!

MRS. LOVETT
You know, dear, it's the strangest thing you coming to
chat with me right now of all moments because, as I was
sitting here with my needles, I was thinking: "What a
good boy Toby is! So hard working, so obedient." And I
thought . . . know how you've always fancied coming
into the bakehouse with me to help bake the pies?

TOBIAS
(*For the first time distracted*)
Oh yes, ma'am. Indeed, ma'am. Yes.

MRS. LOVETT

Well, how about it?

TOBIAS

You mean it? I can help make 'em and bake 'em?
(MRS. LOVETT *kisses him again and, rising,*
starts drawing him back toward the pieshop)

MRS. LOVETT

No time like the present, is there?
(*She leads him through the pieshop into the*
bakehouse)

TOBIAS

(*Looking around*)
Coo, quite a stink, ain't there?

MRS. LOVETT

(*Indicating the trap door*)
Them steps go down to the old cellars and the whiffs
come up, love. God knows what's down there—so moldy
and dark. And there's always a couple of rats gone home
to Jesus.
(*She leads him across to the ovens*)
Now the bake ovens is here.
(*She opens the oven doors. A red glow illumi-*
nates the stage. She closes the doors)

TOBIAS

They're big enough, ain't they?

MRS. LOVETT

Hardly big enough to bake all the pies we sell. Ten dozen
at a time. Always be sure to close the doors properly, like
this.

(*Closes doors. Draws him to the butcher's block
table*)
Now here's the grinder.
> (*She turns its handle, indicating how it oper-
> ates*)

You see, you pop meat in and you grind it and it comes
out here.
> (*Indicates the mouth of the grinder*)

And you know the secret that makes the pies so sweet
and tender? Three times. You must put the meat
through the grinder three times.

TOBIAS

Three times, eh?

MRS. LOVETT

That's my boy. Smoothly, smoothly. And as soon as a
new batch of meat comes in, we'll put you to work.
> (*She starts for the door back into the pieshop*)

TOBIAS
(*Blissful*)
Me making pies all on me own! Coo!
> (*Noticing her leaving*)

Where are you going, ma'am?

MRS. LOVETT

Back in a moment, dear.
> (*At the door she turns, blows him a kiss and
> then goes into the pieshop, slamming the door
> behind her and locking it, putting the key in her
> pocket. TOBIAS, too fascinated to realize he has
> been locked in, starts happily turning the handle
> of the grinder*)

TOBIAS

Smoothly does it, smoothly, smoothly . . .

> (As *he grinds and* MRS. LOVETT *appears at the
> foot of the stairs to the tonsorial parlor, unseen
> by her the* BEADLE *enters the back parlor*)

BEADLE

Mrs. Lovett! Mrs. Lovett!

MRS. LOVETT

> (*Climbing the stairs, looking for* TODD)

Mr. Todd! Mr. Todd!

BEADLE

> (*Notices the harmonium, sits down, and sings
> from a song book, accompanying himself*)

Sweet Polly Plunkett lay in the grass,
Turned her eyes heavenward, sighing,
"I am a lass who alas loves a lad
Who alas has a lass in Canterbury.
'Tis a row dow diddle dow day,
'Tis a row dow diddle dow dee . . ."

MRS. LOVETT

> (*Enters, clapping*)

Oh, Beadle Bamford, I didn't know you were a music
lover, too.

BEADLE

> (*Not rising*)

Good afternoon, Mrs. Lovett. Fine instrument you've
acquired.

MRS. LOVETT

Oh yes, it's my pride and joy.

BEADLE

(Sings, as she watches him uneasily)
Sweet Polly Plunkett saw her life pass,
Flew down the city road, crying,
"I am a lass who alas loves a lad
Who alas has a lass loves another lad
Who once I had
In Canterbury.
'Tis a row dow diddle dow day,
'Tis a row dow diddle dow dee . . ."
(He speaks, leafing through the pages)
Well, ma'am, I hope you have a few moments, for I'm
here today on official business.

MRS. LOVETT

Official?

BEADLE

That's it, ma'am. You see, there's been complaints—

MRS. LOVETT

Complaints?

BEADLE

About the stink from your chimney. They say at night it's
something foul. Health regulations being my duty, I'm
afraid I'll have to ask you to let me take a look.

MRS. LOVETT

(Hiding extreme anxiety)
At the bakehouse?

BEADLE

That's right, ma'am.

MRS. LOVETT
(*Improvising wildly*)

But, it's locked and . . . and I don't have the key. It's
Mr. Todd upstairs—he's got the key and he's not here
right now.

BEADLE

When will he be back?

MRS. LOVETT

Couldn't say, I'm sure.

BEADLE
(*Finds a particular song*)

Ah, one of mother's favorites . . .
(*Sings*)
  If one bell rings in the Tower of Bray,
  Ding dong, your true love will stay.
  Ding dong, one bell today
  In the Tower of Bray . . .
  Ding dong!

TOBIAS
(*Joining in from the bakehouse*)

One bell today in the Tower of Bray . . .
Ding dong!

BEADLE
(*Stops playing*)

What's that?

MRS. LOVETT

Oh, just my boy—the lad that helps me with the pies.

BEADLE

But surely he's in the bakehouse, isn't he?

MRS. LOVETT
(*Almost beside herself*)

Oh yes, yes, of course. But you see . . . he's—well, simple in the head. Last week he run off and we found him two days later down by the embankment half-starved, poor thing. So ever since then, we locks him in for his own security.

BEADLE

Then we'll have to wait for Mr. Todd, won't we?
(*Sings*)
But if two bells ring in the Tower of Bray,
Ding dong, ding dong, your true love will stray.
Ding dong—
(*Speaks*)
Since you're a fellow music lover, ma'am, why don't you raise your voice along with mine?

MRS. LOVETT

All right.

BEADLE
(*Sings*)
If three bells ring in the Tower of Bray . . .
Ding dong!

MRS. LOVETT
(*Another "inspiration"*)

Oh yes, of course! Mr. Todd's gone down to Wapping. Won't be back for hours. And he'll be ever so sorry to miss you. Why, just the other day he was saying, "If only the Beadle would grace my tonsorial parlor I'd give him a most stylish haircut, the daintiest shave—all for nothing." So why don't you drop in some other time and take advantage of his offer?

BEADLE

Well, that's real friendly of him.
(*Immovable, he starts to sing another verse*)
If four bells ring in the Tower of—

MRS. LOVETT

Just how many bells are there?

BEADLE

Twelve.
(*Resumes singing*)
Ding dong!

MRS. LOVETT

Ding dong!

TOBIAS

Ding dong!

BEADLE

Ding dong!

BEADLE, MRS. LOVETT, *and* TOBIAS

Then lovers must pray! . . .
(*During this,* TODD *enters, reacts on seeing the* BEADLE)

MRS. LOVETT

(*With a huge smile of relief*)
Back already! Look who's here, Mr. T., on some foolish

complaint about the bakehouse or something. He wants
the key and I told him you had it. But . . .
(*Coquettishly, to the* BEADLE)
. . . there's no hurry, is there, sir? Why don't you run
upstairs with Mr. Todd and let him fix you up nice and
pretty—there'll be plenty of time for the bakehouse later.

BEADLE
(*Considering*)
Well . . . tell me, Mr. Todd, do you pomade the hair? I
dearly love a pomaded head.

MRS. LOVETT
Pomade? Of course! And a nice facial rub with bay rum
too. All for free!

BEADLE
(*To* TODD)
Well, sir, I take that very kindly.

TODD
(*Bowing to the* BEADLE)
I am, sir, entirely at your—disposal.
(*The two men exit.* MRS. LOVETT *hesitates, then
speaks*)

MRS. LOVETT
Let's hope he can do it quietly. But just to be on the safe
side, I'll provide a little musical send-off.
(*She goes to the harmonium, sits down on the
stool and starts playing and singing a loud verse
of "Polly Plunkett" which continues distantly
during the following. In the bakehouse,* TOBIAS
stands by the grinding machine eating a pie. He

feels something on his tongue, puts a finger in
his mouth and pulls the something out, holding
it up for inspection)

TOBIAS

An 'air! Black as a rook. Now that ain't Mrs. Lovett's 'air.
Oh, well, some old black cow probably.
> *(He continues to eat. He bites on something*
> *else, takes it out of his mouth, looks at it)*

Coo, bit of fingernail! Clumsy. Ugh!
> *(He drops the pie. Bored, he starts around the*
> *room, inspecting. He peers at an unidentifiable*
> *hole in the wall—the chute. He is baffled by it.*
> *As he does so, we hear a strange, shambling,*
> *shuffling sound as if a heavy object is falling*
> *inside the wall.* TOBIAS *spins around just as the*
> *bloody body of the* BEADLE *comes trundling out*
> *of the mouth of the chute.* TOBIAS *screams)*

No! Oh no!
> *(He dashes to the door, tries the handle; it is*
> *locked. He starts beating on it)*

Mrs. Lovett! Mrs. Lovett! Let me out! Let me out!
> *(Wildly he tries to break down the door. It is too*
> *solid for him. Whimpering, he stands paralyzed.*
> *Then he sees the open trap door leading to the*
> *cellar steps. He runs and disappears down them.*
> *In the parlor,* MRS. LOVETT *continues to sing*
> *and play. After a suitable period, she stops)*

MRS. LOVETT

. . . With a row dow diddle dow day.
> *(As she gets up from the harmonium,* TODD *hur-*
> *ries in)*

TODD

It's done.

MRS. LOVETT

Not yet it isn't! The boy, he's guessed.

TODD

Guessed what?

MRS. LOVETT

About Pirelli. Since you weren't here, I locked him in the bakehouse. He's been yelling to wake the dead. We've got to look after him.

TODD
(*Fiercely*)

But the Judge is coming. I've arranged it.

MRS. LOVETT

You—worrying about the bloody Judge at a time like this!
　　(*Grabbing his arm and pulling him toward the door*)
Come on.
　　(*The scene blacks out. Members of the company appear and sing*)

COMPANY
(*Variously*)

The engine roared, the motor hissed,
And who could see that the road would twist?
In Sweeney's ledger the entries matched:
A Beadle arrived, and a Beadle dispatched

To satisfy the hungry god
Of Sweeney Todd,

                              ALL
The Demon Barber of Fleet . . .
Sweeney!
. . . Street.
Sweeney! Sweeney!
Sweeney! Sweeney! Sweeney!
Sweeney!
Sweeeeeneeeeey!

> (*And as they sing the name, they transform themselves into the inmates of Fogg's Asylum, which is now revealed: a huge stone wall and a heavy iron door. Behind the wall, the ragged inmates are crawling, lolling, capering, giggling, shrieking. In the center of them sits* JOHANNA, *her long yellow hair tumbling about her*)

                         INMATES
               (*Intoning, chattering, screaming*)
Sweeeeeeeeeeeeeeeneeeeeeeeeeeeey . . . .
Sweeneysweeneysweeneysweeney . . .

> (*These moans and humming noises continue under the following, occasionally interrupted by little mad birdlike outbursts of song.* MR. FOGG *enters with* ANTHONY *in his wigmaker's disguise. He carries a huge pair of scissors. Behind them is the asylum wall*)

                          FOGG
Just this way, sir.

ANTHONY
You do me honor. Mr. Fogg.

FOGG
I agree it would be to our mutual interest to come to
some arrangement in regard to my poor children's hair.

ANTHONY
Your—children?

FOGG
We are one happy family here, sir, and all my patients
are my children, to be corrected when they're naughty,
and rewarded with a sweetie when they're good. But to
our business.
(*As they enter the inside of the asylum, lights
come up behind the scrim wall revealing the
shadows of the inmates.* MR. FOGG, *as in a
shadow play, grabs one female by the hair, pulling her head up for* ANTHONY's *inspection*)
Here is a charming yellow, a little dull in tone perhaps,
but you can soon restore its natural gleam.
(*He drops the head, moves to a man and grabs
his head up by the hair*)
Now, here! A fine texture for a man and, as you must
know, sir, there is always a discount on the hair of a
male.
(ANTHONY *has been looking around and has
spotted* JOHANNA)

ANTHONY
This one here has hair the shade I seek.

FOGG

Poor child. She needs so much correction. She sings all
day and night and leaves the other inmates sleepless.
(*He goes to* JOHANNA *and tugs her, indignantly
struggling, across the floor toward* ANTHONY, *by
the hair*)
Come, child. Smile for the gentleman and you shall have
a sweetie.
(*He brandishes the scissors*)
Now, where shall I cut?

JOHANNA
(*Sees* ANTHONY)

Anthony!

ANTHONY

Johanna!

FOGG

What is this? What is this?

ANTHONY
(*Drawing his pistol*)

Unhand her!

FOGG

Why you—!
(*Clutching the scissors, he moves resolutely toward* ANTHONY. ANTHONY *backs away a few
steps, but* FOGG *keeps coming*)

ANTHONY

Stop, Mr. Fogg, or I'll fire.

FOGG

Fire, and I will stop.

ANTHONY

I cannot shoot.

> (*Losing his nerve,* ANTHONY *drops the gun which*
> JOHANNA *catches in mid-air.* FOGG *moves toward*
> ANTHONY, *raising the scissors.* JOHANNA, *holding*
> *the gun with both hands, shoots* FOGG, *who*
> *falls. She drops the gun and together she and*
> ANTHONY *run out. Compelled by the energy re-*
> *leased by* FOGG's *death, the lunatics tear down*
> *the wall and rush out of the asylum, spilling*
> *with euphoric excitement onto the street*)

LUNATICS

> (*In three contrapuntal groups*)

City on fire!
Rats in the grass
And the lunatics yelling in the streets!
It's the end of the world! Yes!
City on fire!
Hunchbacks dancing!
Stirrings in the ground
And the whirring of giant wings!
Watch out!
Look!
Blotting out the moonlight,
Thick black rain falling on the
City on fire!
City on fire!
City on fire!

> (*During this, police whistles sound.* ANTHONY
> *and* JOHANNA *are still visible hurrying away,* AN-

THONY *systematically disposing of the wigmaker's costume, tossing the hat off here, the
cloak off there, etc. Throughout,* JOHANNA *is excited and chatty. At one point,* ANTHONY *stops
briefly to reconnoiter nervously*)

JOHANNA
Will we be married on Sunday?
That's what you promised,
Married on Sunday!
(*Pensively*)
That was last August . . .
(*He looks at her unbelievingly*)
Kiss me!
(*He drags her off as the* LUNATICS *reappear, this
time in two groups*)

LUNATICS
City on fire!
Rats in the streets
And the lunatics yelling at the moon!
It's the end of the world! Yes!
City on fire!
Hunchbacks kissing!
Stirrings in the graves
And the screaming of giant winds!
Watch out! Look!
Crawling on the chimneys,
Great black crows screeching at the
City on fire!
City on fire!
City on fire!

(As *they run off, lights come up on the*
bakehouse. TODD, *holding a lantern, and* MRS.
LOVETT *enter, looking around for* TOBIAS)

MRS. LOVETT
(*Sings*)

Toby!
Where are you, love?

TODD

Toby!
Where are you, lad?

MRS. LOVETT
Nothing's gonna harm you . . .

TODD

Toby!

MRS. LOVETT
Not while I'm around . . .

TODD
(*Opening trap door, peering down*)
Toby!

MRS. LOVETT
Where are you hiding?
Nothing's gonna harm you,
Darling . . .

TODD
Nothing to be afraid of, boy . . .
(*Closes the trap door, peers into the darkness*)

MRS. LOVETT
Not while I'm around.

TODD
Toby . . .

MRS. LOVETT
(*She and* TODD *move upstage, where their voices echo*)
Demons are prowling everywhere
Nowadays . . .

TODD
Toby . . .
(*They wander off as the* LUNATICS *run on*)

LUNATICS
City on fire!
Rats in the streets
And the lunatics yelling at the moon!
It's the end of the world! Yes!
(*Lights go down on them and come up on the* BEGGAR WOMAN, *peering off through the darkness as if at the pieshop*)

BEGGAR WOMAN
Beadle! . . . Beadle! . . .
No good hiding, I saw you!
Are you in there still,
Beadle? . . . Beadle? . . .
Get her, but watch it!
She's a wicked one, she'll deceive you
With her fancy gowns

And her fancy airs
And her—
   (*Suddenly shrieking*)
Mischief! Mischief!
Devil's work!
   (*Quietly calling again*)
Where are you, Beadle?
Beadle . . .

(*As she shuffles off toward the pieshop, lights
dim on her and come up on the lunatics*)

LUNATICS

City on fire!
Rats in the streets
And the lunatics yelling at the moon!
It's the end of the world! Good!
City on fire!
Hunchbacks kissing!
Stirrings in the graves
And the screaming of giant winds!
Watch out! Look!
Crawling on the chimneys,
Great black crows screeching at the
City on fire! . . .

(*Light comes up on the tonsorial parlor. It is
empty for a moment, then* ANTHONY *and*
JOHANNA, *who is now dressed in a sailor's uni-
form, enter; music under*)

ANTHONY

Mr. Todd?

JOHANNA

No one here. Where is this Mr. Todd?

ANTHONY

No matter. He'll be back in a moment, for I trust him as I trust my right arm. Wait for him here—I'll return with the coach in less than half an hour.

JOHANNA

But they are after us still. What if they trace us here? Oh, Anthony, please let me come with you.

ANTHONY

No, my darling, there is no safety for you on the street.

JOHANNA

But dressed in these sailor's clothes, who's to know it is I?

ANTHONY

No, the risk is too great.
   (As *she turns away pouting, he sings*)
 Ah, miss,
 Look at me, look at me, miss, oh,
 Look at me please, oh,
 Favor me, favor me with your glance.
 Ah, miss,
 Soon we'll be, soon we'll be gone
 And sailing the seas
 And happily, happily wed
 In France.
   (*She looks at him and smiles*)

BOTH

And we'll sail the world
And see its wonders
From the pearls of Spain
To the rubies of Tibet—

JOHANNA	ANTHONY
And then home.	And then come home to London.
Some day.	Some day.

(They kiss)

ANTHONY

(Starting out)

And I'll be back before those lips have time to lose that
smile.

(He rushes off. Music continues under. JOHANNA
*paces. She sees the barber chair, starts to move
toward it. During this, the* BEGGAR WOMAN *can
be seen below approaching the pieshop. A factory
whistle blows.* JOHANNA *gasps, startled, then
goes to the chair. She sits in it. Her hand moves
to inspect the lever, but before she touches it, the*
BEGGAR WOMAN *approaches, calling)*

BEGGAR WOMAN

Beadle! . . .
Beadle!
Where are you?
Beadle, dear!
Beadle!

JOHANNA
(*Simultaneously, jumping up*)
Someone calling the Beadle! I knew it!
(JOHANNA *looks wildly around, sees the chest,
runs to it and clambers in, closing the lid just as
the* BEGGAR WOMAN *comes shuffling on. Dimly
surveying the room, she mimes opening a window. She then gently picks up an imaginary in-
fant and rocks it in her arms*)

BEGGAR WOMAN
(*Suddenly becoming giddily crazy, sings*)
Beadle deedle deedle deedle deedle dumpling
Beadle dumpling bedeedle deedle deedle
Deedle deedle deedle deedle deedle deedle
Deedle deedle deedle—
(*Without warning, leaping in like a thunder-
bolt,* TODD *appears, the razor in his hand; music
continues*)

TODD
You! What are you doing here?

BEGGAR WOMAN
(*Clutching his arm*)
Ah, evil is here, sir. The stink of evil—from below—from
her!
(*Calling*)
Beadle dear, Beadle!

TODD
(*Looking anxiously out the window for the*
JUDGE)
Out of here, woman.

BEGGAR WOMAN
(*Still clutching his arm*)
She's the Devil's wife! Oh, beware her, sir. Beware of
her. She with no pity . . . in her heart.

TODD
Out, I say!

BEGGAR WOMAN
(*Peering dimly at him, sings*)
Hey, don't I know you, mister?
(*On the street the* JUDGE *approaches the tonso-
rial parlor*)

TODD
(*Seeing him*)
The Judge. I have no time.
(*He turns on the* BEGGAR WOMAN, *slits her
throat, puts her in the chair and releases her
down the chute. The* JUDGE *enters the room.
Music continues under*)

JUDGE
Where is she? Where is the girl?

TODD
Below, your Honor. In the care of my neighbor, Mrs.
Lovett. Thank heavens the sailor did not molest her.
Thank heavens too, she has seen the error of her ways.

JUDGE
She has?

TODD
Oh yes, your lesson was well learned, sir. She speaks only
of you, longing for forgiveness.

JUDGE

And she shall have it. She'll be here soon, you say?

TODD
(*Sings*)

I think I hear her now.

JUDGE

Oh, excellent, my friend!

TODD

Is that her dainty footstep on the stair?

JUDGE
(*Listening*)

I hear nothing.

TODD

Yes, isn't that her shadow on the wall?

JUDGE

Where?

TODD
(*Points*)

There!
(*The* JUDGE *looks, getting excited*)
Primping,
Making herself even prettier than usual—

JUDGE
(*Sings*)

Even prettier . . .

TODD

If possible.

JUDGE
(*Blissful*)

Ohhhhhhh,
Pretty women!

TODD

Pretty women, yes . . .

JUDGE
(*Straightening his coat, patting his hair*)
Quickly, sir, a splash of bay rum!

TODD
(*Indicating the chair*)

Sit, sir, sit.

JUDGE
(*Settling into the chair, in lecherous rapture*)
Johanna, Johanna . . .
(TODD *gets a towel, puts it carefully around
him, moves to pick up a bottle of bay rum*)

TODD

Pretty women . . .

JUDGE

Hurry, man!

TODD

Pretty women
Are a wonder . . .

JUDGE

You're in a merry mood again today, barber.

TODD
(*Joyfully*)

Pretty women!

JUDGE
What we do for
Pretty women!   TODD
                         Pretty women!
   (*During the following,* TODD *smooths bay rum
   on the* JUDGE'S *face, reaching behind him for a
   razor*)

Blowing out their candles   Blowing out their candles
Or combing out their hair— Or combing out their hair,
Then they leave—
Even when they leave you   Even when they leave,
And vanish, they somehow   They still
Can still remain   Are there,
There with you there . . . They're there . . .
   (*Music continues under*)

JUDGE

How seldom it is one meets a fellow spirit!

TODD
(*Smiling down*)

With fellow tastes—in women, at least.

JUDGE

What? What's that?

TODD

The years no doubt have changed me, sir. But then, I

suppose, the face of a barber—the face of a prisoner in
the dock—is not particularly memorable.

JUDGE

(With horrified realization)

Benjamin Barker!

> (The factory whistle blows; the JUDGE in terror
> tries to jump up but TODD slashes his throat, then
> pulls the lever and sends the body tumbling out
> of sight and down the chute. Music continues.
> For a long moment, TODD stands crouched for-
> ward by the chair, exhaling deeply. Then slowly
> he drops to his knees and even more slowly holds
> up the razor, gazing at it. He sings)

TODD

Rest now, my friend,
Rest now forever.
Sleep now the untroubled
Sleep of the angels . . .

> (Suddenly remembering)

The boy.

> (He starts down the stairs. He stops midway,
> remembering his razor)

My razor!

> (He starts back up the steps just as JOHANNA has
> climbed out of the chest. She stands frozen)

You! What are you doing here? Speak!

JOHANNA

Oh, dear. Er—excuse me, sir. I saw the barber's sign. So
thinking to ask for a shave, I—

TODD

When? When did you come in?

JOHANNA

Oh sir, I beg of you. Whatever I have seen, no man shall ever know. I swear it. Oh, sir, please, sir . . .

TODD

A shave, eh?
    (He turns chair toward her)
At your service.

JOHANNA

But, sir . . .

TODD

Whatever you may have seen, your cheeks are still as much in need of the razor as before. Sit, sir. Sit.
  (TODD *sits* JOHANNA *in the chair. As he goes for the razor, simultaneously the factory whistle blows and* MRS. LOVETT *is heard screaming "Die! Die!" from the bakehouse below.* JOHANNA *jumps up and runs out,* TODD *lunges after her, misses her. She runs away.* TODD *pauses; another scream from the bakehouse sends him running down the stairs, and as he disappears into the pieshop, the* COMPANY *appears)*

COMPANY
(Sings)

Lift your razor high, Sweeney!
Hear it singing, "Yes!"
Sink it in the rosy skin
Of righteousness!
  (*Light comes up on the bakehouse.* MRS. LOVETT *is standing in horror by the mouth of the chute*

from which the JUDGE, *still alive, clutches her skirt.* MRS. LOVETT *tries to tug the skirt away from the vise-like grip)*

MRS. LOVETT

Die! Die! God in heaven—die!
> (*The* JUDGE's *fingers relax their grip; he is dead. Panting,* MRS. LOVETT *backs away from him and for the first time notices the body of the* BEGGAR WOMAN. *She pauses)*

You! Can it be? How all the demons of Hell come to torment me!
> (*Looks hastily over her shoulder)*

Quick! To the oven.
> (*She starts to drag the* BEGGAR WOMAN *to the oven as* TODD *enters, runs to her)*

TODD

Why did you scream? Does the Judge still live?

MRS. LOVETT

He was clutching, holding on to my skirt, but now—he's finished.
> (*Continues dragging* BEGGAR WOMAN *to oven)*

TODD

Leave them to me. Open the doors.
> (*He starts to shove her toward the oven)*

MRS. LOVETT
> (*Clutching the* BEGGAR WOMAN's *wrists)*

No!

TODD

Open the doors, I say!
> (*He goes to the* JUDGE, *razor in hand, to be sure he's dead;* MRS. LOVETT, *seeing his attention distracted, runs to the oven.* TODD *sees the* JUDGE *is dead and starts back to the* BEGGAR WOMAN *just as* MRS. LOVETT *opens the oven doors and the light hits the* BEGGAR WOMAN)

MRS. LOVETT
> (*Rushing to him*)

No! Don't touch her!

TODD
> (*Leaning down to pick up the* BEGGAR WOMAN)

What is the matter with you? It's only some meddling old beggar—
> (*A chord of music as he realizes who she is*)

Oh no, oh God . . ."Don't I know you?" she said . . .
> (*Looks up*)

You knew she lived. From the first moment that I walked into your shop you knew my Lucy lived!

MRS. LOVETT

I was only thinking of you!

TODD
> (*Looking down again, sings*)

Lucy . . .

MRS. LOVETT

Your Lucy! A crazy hag picking bones and rotten spuds out of alley ashcans! Would you have wanted to know that was all that was left of her?

TODD
(*Slowly looking up*)

You lied to me.

MRS. LOVETT
(*Sings*)

No, no, not lied at all.
No, I never lied.

TODD
(*To the* BEGGAR WOMAN)

Lucy . . .

MRS. LOVETT

Said she took the poison—she did—
Never said that she died—
Poor thing,
She lived—

TODD

I've come home again . . .

MRS. LOVETT

But it left her weak in the head,
All she did for months was just lie there in bed—

TODD

Lucy . . .

MRS. LOVETT

Should've been in hospital,
Wound up in Bedlam instead,
Poor thing!

TODD

Oh, my God . . .

MRS. LOVETT

Better you should think she was dead.
Yes, I lied 'cos I love you!

TODD

Lucy . . .

MRS. LOVETT

I'd be twice the wife she was!
I love you!

TODD

What have I done? . . .

MRS. LOVETT

Could that thing have cared for you
Like me?
    (TODD *rises, soft and smiling;* MRS. LOVETT *takes
    a step away in panic. Waltz music starts*)

TODD

Mrs. Lovett,
You're a bloody wonder,
Eminently practical and yet
Appropriate as always.
As you've said repeatedly,
There's little point in dwelling on the past.

MRS. LOVETT	TODD
Do you mean it?	No, come here, my love . . .
Everything I did I swear	
I thought	
Was only for the best,	Not a thing to fear,
Believe me!	My love . . .
Can we still be	What's dead
Married?	Is dead.

(TODD *puts his arms around her waist; she starts to relax in her babbling, and they sway to the waltz, her arms around his neck*)

TODD

The history of the world, my pet—

MRS. LOVETT

Oh, Mr. Todd,
Ooh, Mr. Todd,
Leave it to me . . .

TODD

Is learn forgiveness and try to forget.

MRS. LOVETT

By the sea, Mr. Todd,
We'll be comfy-cozy,
By the sea, Mr. Todd,
Where there's no one nosy . . .

(*He waltzes her closer to the oven*)

TODD

And life is for the alive, my dear,
So let's keep living it—!

BOTH

Just keep living it,
Really living it—!
> (*He flings her into the oven. She screams. He slams the doors behind her. Black smoke belches forth. The music booms like an earthquake.* TODD, *gasping, sinks to his knees by the oven doors. Then he rises, moves back to the* BEGGAR WOMAN *and kneels, cradling her head in his arms*)

TODD
(*Sings*)

There was a barber and his wife,
And she was beautiful.
A foolish barber and his wife,
She was his reason and his life.
And she was beautiful.
And she was virtuous.
And he was—
(*Shrugs*)
Naive.
> (TOBIAS *emerges from the cellar, singing in an eerie voice. His hair has turned completely white*)

TOBIAS

Pat-a-cake, pat-a-cake, baker man.
Bake me a cake—
No, no,
Bake me a pie—
To delight my eye,
And I will sigh
If the crust be high . . .
(*Sees* TODD)

Mr. Todd.
>(*Notices the* BEGGAR WOMAN)

It's the old woman. Ya harmed her too, have ya? Ya
shouldn't, ya know. Ya shouldn't harm nobody.
>(*He bends to examine the body;* TODD, *suddenly*
>*aware of someone, pushes him violently aside.*
>*As* TOBIAS *staggers back and recovers his balance,*
>*he notices the razor on the floor, picks it up,*
>*plays with it*)

Razor! Razor! Cut, cut, cut cadougan, watch me grind
my corn. Pat him and prick him and mark him with B,
and put him in the oven for baby and me!
>(*Cuts* TODD's *throat.* TODD *dies across the body*
>*of* LUCY *as the factory whistle blows.* ANTHONY,
>JOHANNA *and* OFFICERS OF THE GUARD *come*
>*running on. Seeing the carnage, they all stop*)

You will pardon me, gentlemen, but you may not enter
here. Oh no! Me mistress don't let no one enter here,
for, you see, sirs, there's work to be done, so much work.
>(*While they watch in horror, he moves to the*
>*grinding machine and slowly starts to turn the*
>*handle*)

Three times. That's the secret. Three times through for
them to be tender and juicy. Three times through the
grinder. Smoothly, smoothly . . .
>(JOHANNA *gives a little cry.* ANTHONY *throws his*
>*arm around her. As the group stands watching,*
>*still in silence,* TOBIAS *continues to grind. Sud-*
>*denly, the trap door slams shut; the light*
>*brightens abruptly,* TOBIAS *steps back, looks up*
>*and sings*)

EPILOGUE

TOBIAS

Attend the tale of Sweeney Todd.
His skin was pale and his eye was odd.

JOHANNA *and* ANTHONY

He shaved the faces of gentlemen
Who never thereafter were heard of again.

POLICEMEN

He trod a path that few have trod,

POLICEMEN, JOHANNA, *and* ANTHONY

Did Sweeney Todd,

ALL

The Demon Barber of Fleet Street.

BEGGAR WOMAN
(*Rising*)

He kept a shop in London town,
Of fancy clients and good renown.

JUDGE
(*Rising*)

And what if none of their souls were saved?
They went to their maker impeccably shaved

BEGGAR WOMAN, JUDGE, *and* POLICEMEN
By Sweeney,
By Sweeney Todd,

ALL
The Demon Barber of Fleet Street.

PIRELLI *and* BEADLE
(*Entering*)
Swing your razor wide, Sweeney!
Hold it to the skies!
Freely flows the blood of those
Who moralize!
(*The rest of the* COMPANY *enters*)

COMPANY
His needs are few, his room is bare.
He hardly uses his fancy chair.
The more he bleeds, the more he lives.
He never forgets and he never forgives.
Perhaps today you gave a nod
To Sweeney Todd,
The Demon Barber of Fleet Street.

WOMEN
Sweeney wishes the world away,
Sweeney's weeping for yesterday,
Hugging the blade, waiting the years,
Hearing the music that nobody hears.
Sweeney waits in the parlor hall,
Sweeney leans on the office wall.

MEN
No one can help, nothing can hide you—
Isn't that Sweeney there beside you?

COMPANY
Sweeney wishes the world away,
Sweeney's weeping for yesterday,
Is Sweeney!
There he is, it's Sweeney!
Sweeney! Sweeney!
    (*Pointing around the theater*)
There! There! There! There!
There! There! There!
    (*Pointing to the grave*)
There!
  (TODD *and* MRS. LOVETT *rise from the grave*)

TODD *and* COMPANY
Attend the tale of Sweeney Todd!
He served a dark and a hungry god!

TODD
To seek revenge may lead to hell,

MRS. LOVETT
But everyone does it, and seldom as well

TODD *and* MRS. LOVETT
As Sweeney,

COMPANY
As Sweeney Todd,
The Demon Barber of Fleet . . .

(They start to exit)

. . . Street!

(The COMPANY *exits.* TODD *and* MRS. LOVETT *are the last to leave. They look to each other, then exit in opposite directions,* MRS. LOVETT *into the wings,* TODD *upstage. He glares at us malevolently for a moment, then slams the iron door in our faces. Blackout)*

ADDENDUM

The following scene was cut from the production during previews for reasons of time. It took place immediately after the scene in St. Dunstan's marketplace (pages 32–54) and is included here because the authors feel it helps particularize the character of Judge Turpin.

(*The lights shift to a room in* JUDGE TURPIN'S *house. The* JUDGE *is in his judicial clothes, a Bible in his hand. In the adjoining room,* JOHANNA *sits sewing*)

JUDGE
(*Sings*)
Mea culpa, mea culpa,
Mea maxima culpa,
Mea maxima maxima culpa!
God deliver me! Release me!
Forgive me! Restrain me! Pervade me!
(*He peers through the keyhole of the door to* JOHANNA'S *room*)
Johanna, Johanna,
So suddenly a woman,
The light behind your window—

It penetrates your gown . . .
Johanna, Johanna,
The sun—I see the sun through your—
                    (*Ashamed, he stops peering*)
No!
God!
Deliver me!
                    (*Sinks to his knees*)
Deliver me!
                    (*Starts tearing off his robes*)
Down!
Down.
Down . . .
    (*Now naked to the waist, he picks up a scourge
    from the table*)
Johanna, Johanna,
I watch you from the shadows.
You sigh before your window
And gaze upon the town . . .
Your lips part, Johanna,
So young and soft and beautiful—
                    (*Whips himself*)
God!
                    (*Again and again, as he continues*)
Deliver me!
Filth
Leave me!
Johanna!
Johanna!
I treasured you in innocence
And loved you like a daughter.
You mock me, Johanna,
You tempt me with your innocence,

You tempt me with those quivering—
          (*Whips himself*)
No!
                    (*Again and again*)
God!
Deliver me!
It will—
Stop—
Now! It will—
Stop—
Right—
Now.
Right—
Now.
Right—
Now . . .
   (*Calm again, having kneed his way over to the
   door, he peers through the keyhole*)
Johanna, Johanna,
I cannot keep you longer.
The world is at your window,
You want to fly away.
You stir me, Johanna,
So suddenly a woman,
I cannot watch you one more day—!
          (*Again whips himself into a frenzy*)
God!
Deliver me!
God!
Deliver me!
God!
Deliver—
                    (*Climaxes*)

God!!
*(Panting, he relaxes; when he is in control again,
he starts to dress)*
Johanna, Johanna,
I'll keep you here forever,
I'll wed you on the morrow.
Johanna, Johanna,
The world will never touch you,
I'll wed you on the morrow!
As years pass, Johanna,
You'll tend me in my solitude,
No longer as a daughter,
As a woman.
                    (He is fully dressed again)
Johanna, Johanna,
I'll hold you here forever then,
You'll keep away from windows and
You'll
Deliver me,
Johanna,
From this
Hot
Red
Devil
With your
Soft
White
Cool
Virgin
Palms . . .
*(Magisterial again, picking up the Bible, he pro-
duces a key and opens the door, the key forgot-
ten, still in the lock.* JOHANNA *jumps up)*

JOHANNA

Father!

JUDGE

Johanna, I trust you've not been near the window again.

JOHANNA

(*During this speech her eyes fall on the key in the lock*)

Hardly, dear father, when it has been shuttered and barred these last three days.

JUDGE

How right I was to insist on such a precaution, for once again he has come, that conscienceless young sailor. Ten times has he been driven from my door and yet . . .

(*Breaks off, gazing at her, smitten with lust*)

How sweet you look in that light muslin gown.

JOHANNA

'Tis nothing but an old dress, father.

JUDGE

But fairer on your young form than wings on an angel . . . oh, if I were to think . . .

JOHANNA

(*Demurely, moving to the door*)

Think what, dear father?

JUDGE

If I were to think you encouraged this young rogue . . .

JOHANNA
(*During this speech, she slips the key from the
lock, hides it in her dress*)
I? A maid trained from the cradle to find in modesty and
obedience the greatest of all virtues? Dear father, when
have you ceased to warn me of the wickedness of men?

JUDGE
Venal young men of the street with only one thought in
their heads. But there are men of different and far higher
breed. I have one in mind for you.

JOHANNA
You have?

JUDGE
A gentle man, who would shield you from all earthly
cares and guide your faltering steps to the sober warmth
of womanhood—a husband—a protector—and yet an
ardent lover too. It is a man who through all the years
has surely earned your affection.
(*Drops to his knees*)

JOHANNA
(*Staggered*)
You?!!!

(*The scene blacks out*)